"This book is a lucid gem and it operationalizes seemingly impractical spiritual insight in a way that's grounded in reality, not clouds of abstractions. The methodology it advocates amounts to a very practical way of peeling away the layers of an onion in the form of our attachments to layers upon layers of purported meaning that keep us attached to the world and to suffering. It makes practical the notions of the likes of Krishnamurti and Socrates in pursuing truth to the end of thought. By definition, once the packaging is discarded only truth remains. This book contains no highfalutin stuff, but a practical stepwise process that anyone can benefit from if they share the commitment."

—ROGIER FENTENER VAN VLISSINGEN
Author of *Closing the Circle: Pursah's Gospel of Thomas and a Course in Miracles*

"Based on his own experiences, insights, and self-discoveries, and inspired to share and help others, the author has developed and clearly laid out for us a simple, step-by-step technique—the 'I Think, Therefore I Lie' (ITTIL) technique—that he himself had been using, a technique that, if followed, will end all suffering and lead to lasting inner peace, no matter the outward circumstance. That, in my book, is everything. And this the author gives us with utmost integrity, gentleness, humor, gratitude, and love."

—LENORE
Student of *A Course in Miracles*

"This book will change your life if you practice the technique it offers. Warren Archer is instantly a new spiritual thought leader.

It is a wonderful contribution to both spiritual and personal growth.

This book gives you the tools that are a powerful way of achieving immediate breakthroughs in your life. The information contained in this book can support you in finding inner peace, emotional balance and let you discover your awesome power."

—JAMES MCKILLOP
Entrepreneur and spiritual teacher

"In the words of Kabir: *Every thought has a counter thought. And as Sri Ramana says: In vain is this discussion between duality and nonduality.*

Warren Archer has spoken from realization, covers the distance, and makes a credible offering."

—AMITABH DIVAKAR
Author of OM Within

"Everyone would be better off reading this book. Mr. Archer's technique for awakening in the present moment serves particularly well for both pragmatists and logicians. I cannot recommend this text highly enough to those who are tired of seeking answers that science, philosophy can never offer, but will only accept ideas that are logically derived, and therefore hold up to all scrutiny. Any questions raised while reading have been foreseen and addressed by the author well in advance of the final chapter."

—A. ZAVITZIANOS
Mathematician and programmer

"In this stimulating and provocative book, Warren Archer offers a simple and effective technique for freedom from suffering by eliminating belief in thoughts. Easy to read and full of exciting ideas, it opens a new, if controversial, vista on how to think constructively."

—PROFESSOR LOUKA T. KATSELI
Former Minister of Economy of Greece

"This book lives up to the promise of its provocatively original title. It targets the restless reasoning of the ego mind, which endlessly churns out the thoughts 'that you think you think' (*A Course in Miracles*), in its frantic efforts to understand and control a world based on the illusion of separation. The book artfully engages the conditioned mind in a gentle but thorough scrutiny of its own thoughts, thereby exposing fundamental flaws in its core beliefs. ITTIL offers a simple, powerful technique that, if practiced, results in freedom from the deadening weight of a thought system predicated on fear, leaving the mind open to discover all manner of wonderful things."

—PAULA DA SILVA
Metaphysician

I Think, Therefore I Lie

I THINK,
THEREFORE I LIE

A Radical Technique for Awakening Now

WARREN ARCHER

FOREWORD BY GUY BRILANDO

Stingheart Press

ARIZONA

SECOND EDITION

10 8 7 6 5 4 3 2

Library of Congress Control Number: 2018906718

Hardcover ISBN-13: 978-0-9896232-4-7
Paperback ISBN-13: 978-0-9896232-9-2
Audiobook ISBN: 978-0-9896232-7-8
Ebook ISBN: 978-0-9896232-8-5

Cover designers: Laura Duffy, Eric Hubbel
Book designer: Karen Minster
Copyeditors: Rachelle Mandik, 1st edition
Debra Nichols, 2nd edition
Proofreader: Debra Nichols

StingHeartPress

For Dad

CONTENTS

FOREWORD

I Think, Therefore I Lie penetrates into the depths of those mysterious beliefs that control us—first and foremost negatively, but—as you are about to explore—also those positive beliefs that, likewise, can and do bring suffering.

I first met Warren on October 31, 2008, while flying for our airline. We were locked inside the flight deck for hours over a period of several days. Warren and I were captivated with fascinating conversation as we swapped stories and with our mutual desire to help others. Warren immediately struck me as one of the most intelligent people I'd ever met. He's a standout among the unusually high number of successful people I've been associated with over the years.

It was Warren's calm demeanor, innate intellect, and his deep thinking that captured my attention. As we conversed, he began taking an interest in my own personal journey of transformation that led to working with others and achieving prodigious results. From this common thread, he expressed his concept, "I Think, Therefore I Lie." Utterly intrigued, I was also in awe of his mastery of thinking, philosophy, and the logic he expressed. He so inspired me, that I eventually gained the courage and journeyed down my own path of publishing a book to help others evolve beyond their circumstances.

Fortunately, *you* don't have to be locked behind a closed door to absorb his fascinating insight! Purposeful—while driving toward perfection—Warren's tireless efforts are now here for all of us to learn and grow from. You are free to rapidly attain his amazing discernment with these pages before you. Prepare to be unleashed and released from all self-inflicted torment and the search for something that is already with you right here and now!

This is more than just words on paper. This book is a deliverance from your unnecessary suffering and seeking. How? As Warren states, the whole point of the ITTIL technique is to use thoughts as a tool instead of letting them use you—if you find them useful, without believing in them. My takeaway? It is a book of awakening and detachment from most unrecognized beliefs that control us, which all too often lead to unnecessary suffering.

Furthermore, Warren takes his concept beyond the explanatory. He expresses the practicality of the ITTIL technique through his own exceptional perseverance and adversities, including a brush with death. Concurrently, he provides authentic life happenings that we all experience, and breaks down his exclusive technique of releasing suffering step by step. Through an abundance of examples, you are about to be guided (in an easy-to-follow format) on how to live a happier, more stress-free, suffering-free life. Take your time with this material. Digest the concepts, then *practice* and put *into* practice this unique technique exactly as explained and you will be astounded with the results you experience.

Guy Brilando
Author of *Discovering Your Authentic Truth*

I Think, Therefore I Lie

1.
The End of Suffering

BELIEVE IT OR NOT

It all happened in less than a minute.

I was sitting in the front row, with the bulkhead of the Airbus 321 cabin separating me from first class. To my right, a businesswoman was pecking at her laptop keyboard.

I was going to do some writing as well—fine-tuning the outline for my second novel.

I was hoping to finish the first draft of my manuscript—maybe even have something ready for my editor—by the time I returned from that trip.

I figured I'd be gone a week. Maybe a little longer, depending on how my father was feeling. I hadn't seen him in three years, and I'd planned on visiting him with my family five weeks later, for his eighty-fifth birthday. Hopping over to Greece with a mere seven hours' lead time had not been in my plans, but due to his deteriorating health, I'd known for some time that I might have to travel there on short notice.

It was then that the flight attendant made the standard pre-pushback PA instructing us to turn off all electronic devices or put them in airplane mode.

I had my finger on the screen, about to swipe left, when I heard the sound of an incoming email.

It read as follows (names withheld):

L— just told me that dad died five minutes ago. They will take
his body to the hospital church now. That's where I'm going.
Love,
D—

For more than a decade, I'd imagined the moment I'd hear of my
father's death.

I had assumed my initial reaction would be far more subdued,
with long-term effects not dissimilar to what I'd experienced back
when I was fifteen and I'd overheard my classmates saying that my
friend Jan had been hit by a train.

That news had resulted in two years of self-inflicted psychological torture that led to a series of autoimmune diseases.

Sitting there, behind the bulkhead of the jet, the beginnings of
all that suffering I'd gone through with the death of my friend were
there in their entirety—I could *feel* it, just as I'd foreseen, all in that
short space of time.

The first feeling I recall was a blast of unreality, as though I were
watching a movie in which I was a character trapped in an improb-
able script that stretched credibility for even the most naïve of audi-
ences.

Shit! I didn't shout the word—I'm fairly certain about that—but
it sure felt as though I had.

I shot a glance at the lady next to me. She was in the process
of saving her spreadsheet and closing her MacBook. She didn't even
look in my direction.

Nobody seemed to have noticed or cared, which was a good
thing, because I was traveling in my pilot's uniform.

My next thought was: What was my brother thinking? Why
would he tell me this in an email?

I heard the whine of the number-two engine spinning.

Why the hell didn't he *call* me?

Why did Dad have to die *now*? Three years and he'd been doing just fine. Giving talks, interviews on TV, and only a few months earlier, he'd published his second book. All he had to do was hold on for five measly weeks and he would have seen me and my family, including his youngest grandson, who'd just turned four.

There were all these things I wanted to tell him.

And there were the books I'd write that he'd never read.

I should never have listened to their advice to delay the trip. They said I'd be sending him a message that I didn't believe he was going to make it. They said I'd demoralize him by visiting. And I'd listened. That had been *my* doing. . . .

I could have seen him. I could have paid attention to the warning signs. To what my mother had been telling me for months: "Don't wait, *go*. Go see him now."

A new feeling came to me. That sense of hopeless irreversibility that comes with loss. A longing for the impossible. That *if-only* thought.

I'd been practicing the ITTIL technique (much more on this later) for several years at that point, but when it came to me, inside the one-minute mark, it hit me with tsunami force, blasting away the remnants of what was crushing me.

In that instant of letting go, I was spun around 180 degrees, propelled from the vortex of dark emotions and the promise of years of suffering, to a peace, an expanding love, and a gratitude that resides nowhere, that abides nowhere, and is utterly beyond words.

DEALING WITH SUFFERING

In the airplane, before I got the news, I was thinking about the outline for my novel—I was focused, in the groove, in the flow, in the moment.

I was happy.

All that collapsed when I read the email from my brother.

Happy one moment, devastated the very next.

While this is an extreme case, we've all experienced similar situations and similar feelings.

When I use the word "suffering," I'm referring to all kinds of suffering, not just the obvious, dramatic kind. I'm referring to a suffering that comes in all shapes and sizes. From depression, anger, grief, humiliation, and guilt, to impatience, irritability, and even plain old boredom.

We've all suffered in some way or another. Looking back at our lives, how much of it was spent waiting, hoping, feeling uncomfortable, and being bored? Happiness happens for most of us, but it isn't the norm. It arises as little bubbles, rarely as big explosions.

Most of us experience the mid-range of suffering as the enduring background of our experience, with brief moments of happiness and unhappiness defining the peaks and troughs.

Taking a closer look at the times you remember being happy, how much of that time were you *really* happy? How much of it was trying to hold on to the moment that had just passed or looking forward to something more in the moments that were to come? How much of what you call happiness was really a longing for what once was or what you hope will be?

When you look at it in this way, the periods of happiness are few and far between, and most of life in the waking state is seen as some expression of suffering.

Most of us consider suffering a normal part of life—the price we pay for happiness. Because we can't be happy all the time, right? This is a common view of suffering, but it doesn't typically give rise to an acceptance of suffering. Instead, it's a form of apathy that arises after countless failed attempts to alleviate suffering.

Suffering seems to be a fundamental human problem.

No matter what form it takes (boredom, sadness, depression, anxiety, anger), all suffering is characterized by some degree of resistance to the present moment.

The characteristics of suffering are not the cause of suffering, and the problem of suffering lies in the misidentification of its cause.

We believe our suffering comes from situations external to ourselves.

Adopting this typical perspective, in the story at the beginning of this chapter, it would seem the cause of my suffering was the news that my father had died.

HOW WE USUALLY HANDLE SUFFERING

The misidentification of the cause of suffering results in a futile effort to make ourselves feel better by solving the wrong problem.

There are several ways we typically deal with suffering.

Subtraction

The subtraction approach involves trying to alleviate suffering by eliminating the cause and is more common for those of us who endure intense suffering, especially for long periods of time. Although this approach is the closest to the mark, it typically misses because most of us don't actually know the cause of our suffering.

Resignation

Resignation is not some deep spiritual acceptance of what is. It's a false kind of acceptance. This outlook typically embraces the idea that there is nothing that can be done about suffering. It's a given. It's fate and the victim has simply been dealt a lousy hand of cards. People who adopt this approach view themselves as victims of their suffering. The only upside is the possibility of being comforted by others who validate their suffering.

Addition

Addition is the most common approach to suffering. It is addition in the sense of seeking more happiness to add to our lives. We seek things that we believe will make us happy. This happiness could come in the form of quick fixes—entertainment of various kinds. We might go to a concert, the movies, our favorite restaurant. Other quick fixes might come in a bottle, or in a needle. It might come as sex or gambling or any of the uncountable addictive vices.

Another way addition deals with suffering is through long-term goals. People might seek fame, fortune, or any goal they believe will give them some kind of lasting happiness that would eliminate—or at least overshadow—their suffering.

For a handful of us, that long-term goal is enlightenment.

I put enlightenment in the category of addition because that's how most seekers view it, at least in the beginning, once they've started on the path. They see it more as permanent, lasting happiness rather than as the end of suffering.

WHY THESE APPROACHES
TO SUFFERING FAIL

Whether people try subtraction, resignation, or addition, they typically don't find relief from suffering; all they manage to do is change the nature of their suffering.

With subtraction, people try to eliminate their suffering by dealing with what they perceive to be its cause. This is the most logical approach of them all.

While subtraction is the most logical and direct of the three approaches, it rarely succeeds. This is simply because of a misdiagnosis of the problem. When a doctor treats the wrong thing, at best there may be temporary relief with no harm done, however the underlying problem remains. The disease or disorder will rise again.

No matter how good a surgeon is, if she's operating on the wrong part of the body, the operation will not be effective.

The majority of people who try to alleviate their suffering don't know the cause. As a result, their suffering continues. This can be frustrating and downright scary. After years, perhaps decades of trying, this might lead to giving up, which may come in the form of moving on to the resignation approach, or something like it, or even the ultimate act of giving up—suicide.

Let's say someone is in what they perceive to be a bad relationship. She's suffering. The cause of her suffering is believed to be the relationship. The subtraction solution would be to eliminate the cause: the relationship. Stopping all communications, leaving, ending the relationship. Perhaps temporarily suspending relationships of that nature altogether. This may provide some degree of relief from her suffering, but since the cause of the suffering was misidentified as the other person, the relief will be short-lived. At some point she will find that wherever she goes, no matter how final the end seemed to be—even if it's sanctioned by a court of law—she is carrying the relationship with her in her thoughts. There's no escaping it. No subtracting the relationship.

Addition doesn't work either, at least not in the long run. No matter how many ways people try to find happiness, if the underlying suffering has not been eliminated, that suffering will dominate their experience. Money, fame, fortune, relationships, addictive behaviors, or any other pursuit will not bring lasting happiness, only the transitory variety. They never completely mask the underlying problem of suffering.

Addition is the most prevalent solution. We see it all the time in movies. People going to bars to "drown their sorrows" after a breakup, losing their job, or whatever form that sorrow takes. They add alcohol to the problem. The alcohol drowns the thoughts by dulling them to the point where they have less of a hold. But the next day, the suffering comes back full force, and this time with a hangover.

In the example of the perceived bad relationship, an addition solution would be to jump from one relationship to another. While in the honeymoon phase of the new relationship, this solution may appear to have worked, but once the courtship is over, the same old problems will likely return. She may think, "Did I find the wrong person? *Again?* How could this be happening?" Or perhaps the same problems don't come back, but now there are completely new problems. Either way, the suffering was not quelled in the new relationship. It was put to sleep for a short while, but the suffering was always there.

Some people dedicate themselves to their work to drown their suffering. I've done this myself. As long as I was focused on my work, on what I was doing—whether it was flying, writing a novel, or practicing the piano—it seemed I was keeping the suffering at bay. The problem typically arose when it was bedtime and all the distracting activity had settled down. Then the suffering would come back, and with a vengeance. That's when the house felt emptier than ever and the futility of trying to add happiness to fix the problem made itself blatantly apparent.

All things added in order to "make you happy" have a tendency to become addictive, because the relief from suffering they offer is always only temporary. What we all want is *permanent* relief, not a quick fix, and therefore a little is never enough.

Those who deal with suffering through resignation and turn themselves into victims in order to elicit attention are swimming in a pool of the very thing they are trying to avoid. The attention is addictive in the beginning. But like any addiction, more and more is needed to get a satisfactory fix and find relief from suffering. In the case of using suffering to get attention, the more this happens, the more it fails because with the passage of time, the story loses its novelty. This suffering identity that has been created then has to be maintained, and in order to do so, the suffering itself has to be maintained.

It becomes a competition for attention. One's suffering has to be greater than that of other people, otherwise they'll lose attention to those whose suffering is perceived to be greater.

It is also harder for these people to step out of and abandon the story surrounding their suffering because now they've committed some part—and in many cases, a significant part—of their identity to this story.

I used to do a version of this when I was suffering with nobody around whom I would want to share it with. I'd be in some "unreal" situation that I felt certain would get me plenty of attention. I remember being in the hospital. The nurse was incapable of finding a good vein for the IV. She tried again and again, disregarding my advice to steer clear of my left arm. While this was all happening, I was working on my story. I adjusted it according to the person I was imagining I'd be telling it to. Like when I was working on a novel, I'd look for ways to make my story more powerful. The better the story, the more attention I'd get. This was one way I'd cope with my suffering in the moment, focusing on how I'd tell people about it later. Most of the time, as with this instance, I never ended up telling anyone. Playing victim was out of character for me, but telling myself I would relay my story offered me some degree of comfort as it gave me the illusion of not being alone and of being able to share my experience.

The resignation reaction to suffering has the advantage of a seemingly unlimited supply of stories of suffering. And when people are in that mode and habitually use their suffering to get attention, they tend to make a self-fulfilling prophecy of their lives, making their victimhood into something that appears very real.

But this doesn't do anything to alleviate suffering in the long run. It actually increases suffering and makes an addiction out of it.

Let us go back to the story of my learning of my father's death, but from the perspective of the three typical approaches to suffering.

In the beginning, I was completely focused on my writing. Assuming suffering had not been eliminated—and in my case, it hadn't—this kind of activity constituted a form of addition. It could be highly effective in the moment, but it only worked while I was completely focused. Once that focus was lost, whatever suffering remained would resurface.

I lost my focus when I read the email from my brother. Reactivity took over. A reaction that I'd rehearsed for many years, just by thinking about that very moment over and over again.

My immediate reaction to dealing with the suffering, therefore, was resignation. I saw myself as a victim of the circumstance of my father's death.

I perceived the problem to be outside myself. In perceiving the situation in this manner, I relegated control to the situation. I was a puppet of circumstance. In a world where suffering and happiness are dictated by situations, I could be considered an unlucky person. Unlucky for losing a father before I'd had a proper chance to say goodbye. Unlucky because most of my family insisted I not go and visit him earlier. There were a host of reasons to support my negative belief.

Resignation was not my usual reaction of choice, but in this case, I didn't have much of an alternative. After all, what was there to subtract? How could I make the situation better?

If the ITTIL technique hadn't kicked in and eradicated my suffering, given time and a chance to adjust to the shock of the knowledge that my father was dead, I would most likely have used addition to address my pain.

This addition would have probably entailed a rather intense focus on my writing and piano practice. Doing so had helped me deal with suffering prior to that event, and I would have reasoned that if I could take my attention off his death for long enough, time would heal my suffering to the point where I'd be able to face up to the situation and then move on.

Whatever the suffering, whether it's as major as grieving or as minor as restlessness, the natural tendency is to defend against it somehow—be it by subtraction, resignation, or addition.

There is actually a fourth approach to dealing with suffering, and it is a less common one. This approach seeks freedom from suffering, lasting happiness, truth, or specifically, the one thing I used to imagine encapsulated all of these—enlightenment.

After suffering "one damned thing after another," you may have come to the realization that something inside yourself is suffering. It cannot be the situation. If situations cause suffering, then solving the problem of suffering is hopeless, because fixing a situation only provides temporary relief from suffering. Pretty soon—give it a couple of hours, days, or weeks—a new situation will invariably arise that will trigger suffering all over again.

Where all other solutions have failed, the last solution remains one that reigns supreme and offers genuine hope of freedom from suffering. That solution is enlightenment. Many people believe that if somehow they could become enlightened, they'd gain not just lasting but *permanent* happiness.

In almost every case, this approach fails. The reason is that you cannot add happiness in the hopes of somehow neutralizing unhappiness. In fact, happiness attracts its opposite—unhappiness—because the peak creates the trough!

This last approach fails for other reasons as well. Enlightenment is an especially tricky goal. After all, how can you know what enlightenment is until you have actually attained it? And if you don't know what enlightenment is, how can you possibly hope to attain it? How can you head for a destination when you don't know where that destination is? Furthermore, how can you know that enlightenment is a destination in the first place?

These are just a few problems that pop up for seekers of enlightenment. But there's more.

By pursuing enlightenment, you are rejecting the present in favor of something "better" in the imagined future. So, ironically, the pursuit of enlightenment itself makes it unattainable, since for as long as you hope for enlightenment in your future, it will never come. It cannot come, because by definition, the future is never now and if you do not accept what is, how could there ever be a time where you would accept that you are enlightened?

These are the problems I faced when I started my quest to end my suffering by attaining enlightenment.

But it wasn't in my nature to give up. I was stubborn and determined. In fact, the harder the goal, the greater my motivation. If enlightenment existed, and other people had attained what I considered to be the loftiest of goals, then I was determined to do so as well. Little did I know then where this pursuit would lead.

HOW THE ITTIL TECHNIQUE WAS BORN

At age sixteen, after a year of grieving my friend's death, I started Transcendental Meditation (TM), which I believed would not only alleviate my intense suffering but would also lead to enlightenment.

TM didn't seem to be getting me enlightened, however, so I continued the practice but searched elsewhere for enlightenment.

But, not knowing exactly what enlightenment was, I had no metric to gauge if I was progressing, or how fast I was progressing, and therefore if the path I was on was the right path for me or not.

The active pursuit of enlightenment came to a painful, grinding halt after a year of extensive reading of Krishnamurti.

He didn't offer a technique; he merely negated all paths and repeatedly referred to inquiry without explaining how this was to be done, thereby killing any hope I had of becoming enlightened. Desperate, I went to Zurich, Switzerland, to speak with Elisabeth Haich. She told me I'd become enlightened, but I'd choose a difficult path. Her gentle companion and caretaker, Yogi Yesudian, took me on a walk, and said I should not abandon my quest for enlightenment, and that Krishnamurti was not the right teacher for me.

Despite the advice, because I perceived Krishnamurti's words as negative, I felt they were somehow true. *I believed that what was painful and pessimistic was truer than what was pleasant and hopeful.* As a result, I decided to postpone my quest indefinitely. Instead of enlightenment, I pursued various career goals: becoming a classical pianist, a novelist, and finally an airline pilot.

Years later, in the summer of 1998, at a hotel in Italy known as Villa di Papà (the pope's villa), I had a short period of clarity like nothing I'd ever experienced before.

I woke up after a deep sleep, feeling like I was floating. I found myself getting out of bed and walking to the middle of the small room as if I were exploring some alien landscape.

It was like watching a 3-D movie in which I was the only actor.

I questioned the concept of time, and I immediately saw a graphic representation of the thought—a straight cyan line, similar to a light-saber, but only half the diameter of a pencil.

This didn't seem quite right, so the line snaked around my waist, becoming a glowing Hula-Hoop.

That was a better rendition, but still incomplete. As if in response to what I was thinking, the hoop became two, and then fanned out into countless hoops until I was engulfed in a translucent cyan sphere of light.

Somehow I knew two things: first, I could answer any question that came to me; second, this experience would not last long.

For every question I asked, I posed a corresponding opposite question.

For each question, the answer that arose was a resounding "Yes!"

During this experience, the paradox these answers generated did not disturb me in the least. Afterward, however, and for many years, I was somewhat confused, because if everything were true, then the statement that everything was not true was also true!

I sensed that the solution to my quest was in finding a way to see everything as untrue. This would resolve the problem of doubt, because there'd be no belief to doubt!

However, in trying to see that all my thoughts were not true, I ran into yet another challenge: I couldn't reconcile this statement with thoughts such as the one that said there was a large, solid rock in front of me.

Fifteen years went by before I came across the contemporary philosopher Greg Goode, whose logic and clarity resonated deeply with me. Through him, I learned about what is known as the Direct Path and direct-path inquiry (reliance on what is perceived, rather than what is conceived). He also introduced me to the work of the famous eighteenth-century philosopher George Berkeley.

With the help of Berkeley's immaterialism and with the Direct Path, I was able to return to the idea that all thoughts are untrue.

I Think, Therefore I Lie was born.

The practical application of this—the ITTIL (I Think, Therefore I Lie) technique—came shortly thereafter, and for several years, I began using it on my thoughts. At first, I used the ITTIL technique on more-subjective thoughts, such as the one that said I was too fat. I progressed from that to using it on deeper-rooted thoughts that I considered more objective and practical, such as those that identified me by age, sex, name, and profession.

With the help of ITTIL, a thought can be used or dropped at any given moment with no downside.

The clutter of useless thoughts gives way to one beneficial thought at a time, and the noise of circular thinking becomes a thing of the past.

What's left is freedom from suffering.

THE ITTIL TECHNIQUE
AND THE END OF SUFFERING

Freedom from suffering comes from
using thoughts without believing them.

I realize that for some readers, this might be too radical a concept to swallow in the beginning, and so we will return to it in later chapters. For now it is enough to know that there is a technique for eliminating your suffering in the present moment.

At any given time, if you want freedom from suffering, there's the ITTIL technique. If you prefer suffering, you can continue believing your thoughts and the story they are telling you.

Which will you choose? ITTIL or suffering? Every moment, the decision is simple.

You are awake and free from suffering until the moment you believe. If you believe, you apply ITTIL, and the practice of removing belief drops the veil of delusion, awakens you to the present moment, and ends your suffering now.

In the beginning, there may be the illusion that this awakening is a choice: You either practice the ITTIL technique or you don't.

Eventually, you will see there was never a choice. There was awakening or there was belief in a story. However, once the story is clearly seen as untrue, belief in the story can be automatically dropped. *There is no way to believe what you know to be a lie.*

There is nothing to decide when it comes to choosing freedom from suffering over suffering. In that sense, there is no choice.

A BEFORE-AND-AFTER STORY

Before the ITTIL Technique

Almost two decades ago, I was in a hotel trying to fall asleep. Somehow, my attention went to my breathing. My chest felt heavy. I became very aware that I was breathing, and I had the thought that if I stopped thinking about breathing, I'd stop breathing and I would die in the agony of suffocation.

Suddenly, my chest tightened, and I felt a pain that was exactly like what they describe as the experience of a heart attack.

I sat up, clutching my chest.

It felt like a ton of bricks was crushing me, and each and every breath was a struggle.

My modem was plugged in. I waited for my laptop to dial the number and exchange those characteristic static sounds with the server while it established a connection with the internet.

They didn't have that much information available on the internet back then, but the Yahoo! search engine did come up with a list of symptoms of a heart attack.

The first item on the list was chest pain or pressure, and I had that in spades.

The second item was the feeling of suffocating. The feeling that your upper torso is being squeezed or crushed.

Oh dear God, did I have that.

Shortness of breath. Yes, yes, and *hell* yes.

At this point, I was asking myself if I would have time to call for an ambulance.

Other symptoms included sweating, fatigue, coughing, and a racing heart.

I skipped through those because I had already hit the important symptoms, and it didn't matter to me that I wasn't feeling the rest. After all, I didn't need to have all the symptoms to be having a heart attack.

The website warned me to call for help immediately.

As terrified as I was, that warning gave me pause.

If I were really dying of a heart attack, would it matter if I called for an ambulance? How could they possibly get to me in time?

If I wasn't having a heart attack, then how the hell would I explain myself? "I'm not a hypochondriac, I swear, it's just that I . . ."

I went back to my search results and saw "panic attack."

I read through the symptoms. I was shocked to find that I fit the bill for those as well.

But there was nothing wrong with my head. I wasn't suffering from depression or anything like that. Life was fine, just as it always was. I wasn't the worrying type. That is to say, I didn't worry about things of no significance.

I had a logical thinking process and I wouldn't be susceptible to something as lame as a panic attack . . . right?

Either way, all websites seemed to agree that if I was unsure about my situation, I should seek immediate medical attention.

I looked at another website on panic attacks and that's when I read the following:

"Nobody ever dies of a panic attack."

All at once, I noticed my symptoms were gone.

Just like that.

But it could have been a coincidence. I could have had a minor heart attack and it just happened to have ended when I read those words. One couldn't be too careful.

So I arranged to see a cardiologist. He did a stress test and said I had the heart of a twenty-year-old.

This satisfied me . . . for a while.

Then I read that stress tests often miss serious heart conditions and that some people who were given a clean bill of health following such tests had died of congestive heart failure. They had a small blockage of the heart artery, but it ruptured and formed a clot. Only an angiogram could detect such a blockage, but angiograms were themselves risky procedures because they could *cause* a heart attack, a stroke, kidney damage, or damage to the catheterized artery.

Logic prevailed, and I decided against having an angiogram.

I had a few panic attacks after that, and so over a period of three years, I'd visited half a dozen cardiologists.

All of them said I had nothing to worry about, but for a long while, that didn't keep me from worrying.

After the ITTIL Technique

One night, a year or so after discovering the ITTIL technique, just before sleeping, my attention found its way to my breathing just as it had many years before, and I felt an abrupt tightening in my chest.

I applied the ITTIL technique on the thought I was believing and rested patiently with the physical experience I was having. It didn't last more than fifteen seconds.

There was no fear with the experience, just a sense of fascination. I remember thinking, Hmm. That's interesting. There it is again. How long can this last without belief?

It turned out, not long. Not long at all.

What's more, there was no sense of wanting the experience to go away. Instead, there was a thrill in observing how things work now with the ITTIL technique—what I imagine it would be like testing a superpower.

FULFILLMENT ACTION

This is not the ITTIL technique; consider this fulfillment action a fun warm-up.

It is important that you do the end-of-chapter fulfillment actions and not simply read through them or skip them, because they serve to prepare you for chapter 5, where you will start practicing the ITTIL technique itself.

Find Your Suffering

Because you're presently in a position where you're reading a book, it's unlikely that you're experiencing extreme suffering or anything as obvious as depression, sadness, grief, guilt, or anger, otherwise, at this very moment, presumably you wouldn't be engaged in an activity such as reading, you'd be seeking help from a therapist or some other expert.

If you can't find any obvious signs of suffering right now, then for the purpose of this fulfillment action, remember a time when you were suffering from some negative emotion.

Find the Thought

What causes suffering is a thought you're believing in the moment.

This fulfillment action is to identify the thought.

Generally speaking, the more extreme the suffering, the easier it is to identify the belief that is causing it.

How do you know you've found the thought?

If the thought you come up with seems to trigger the feeling you identified as your past suffering, then you know you've got it.

Sometimes narrowing down the thought by adjusting a word or two in the statement does the trick.

Wherever possible, when finding the thought that is causing your suffering, modify it into a direct statement and not a negation.

For example, "I'm not good at this," could be modified to "I'm bad at this."

Note: *Do not make this change to the original statement if doing so causes it to resonate less.*

For example, if the modification of "I'm bad at this" really doesn't feel true to you, whereas "I'm not good at this" does feel true, and you can't find an alternative, then keep the statement as you originally had it.

Finding Opposites

Finding the opposite thought to the one that you're believing is simple, but often attaining simplicity necessitates practice, because we humans have the tendency to make things much more complicated than they need to be.

All you need to do to find the opposite is insert the word "not."

So if the thought is "This is bad."

The opposite thought would be "This is *not* bad."

That may seem obvious, but many people would be inclined to say that the opposite of bad is good and therefore the opposite thought would be "This is good."

There is a subtle but very important distinction between the two. The ITTIL technique negates the truth of the original statement; it doesn't seek an alternative truth. "This is not bad" is a negation of "This is bad," whereas "This is good" is an entirely different statement altogether because it's a statement without negation and is therefore suggestive of a truth.

This is not merely semantics, although it could probably be seen as such; it's simply how the ITTIL technique works.

Find the opposite of the following statements:

"I am fat."

Easy, right?

The correct answer is "I am *not* fat."

But how about finding the opposite of the following (and now we will see why avoiding negations in the original statements makes things easier):

"I am not good enough."

Or this: "I am not smart."

A computer would have no problem with this. It would simply follow instructions and come up with the following opposites:

- "I am *not* not good enough."
- "I am *not* not smart."

A human might come up with the easier sounding:

- "I am good enough."
- "I am smart."

As far as the ITTIL technique goes, however, the computer would be right.

To make it easier on the ears, emphasize the first *not*. So "I am **not** not good enough," and "I am **not** not smart."

I'll explain later on why this is so important, but for now, suffice it to say that in order for the ITTIL technique to work, all thoughts must be treated as *equally* untrue, and so the opposite thought should only serve to negate the original thought, not become a substitute belief.

If it were okay to say that the opposite of bad is good, then "good" could easily become a substitute belief. This is not as likely to happen if we use a statement that is a negation, in this case, "*not* bad."

2.
What Lies in Thought

CERTAIN DEATH

I was shivering in my paper-thin hospital gown with nothing more than a rudimentary white cover between me and what felt like a meat locker.

When my sonographer finally returned, there were four doctors with her.

None of them said a single word to me, though I noticed them stealing a glance in my direction every now and then.

They'd gathered behind a glass control-room window and I could see them huddled over images, intense concentration in their faces. This lasted for almost an hour, and before I was carted off to the hallway in the mobile hospital bed, I asked the sonographer the question that I'd been pondering since the moment she'd started the exam at least two hours earlier: "What's going on?"

She replied with an ominous question: "How did your surgeon know?" She mentioned him by name.

"Know what?"

"That you have a blood clot," she replied, as if that should have been obvious.

Hospital transportation must have been overworked that day, because I waited on my bed for more than an hour in that brightly lit corridor. Doctors, as well as other patients in wheelchairs and mobile hospital beds pushed by me. I might as well have been invisible. There was no one to talk to.

I was going to die. I felt like a man walking down death row, a priest at my side, the electric chair just around the corner.

My imminent death was certain. What was not certain was how much time there was before the clot got to my brain or my heart and ended my life.

How was I certain? Less than five days earlier, I'd been at the surgeon's office as he was explaining the risks and details of the splenectomy he would perform.

I was a seasoned abdominal-surgery patient and wasn't in the least worried about the surgery itself. My concern was whether the operation would cure my hemolytic anemia. It had a 25 percent success rate, and I wasn't delighted with these odds, especially considering that none of the medications I'd tried up to that point had worked to prevent my autoimmune system from killing off my red blood cells.

The surgeon had come highly recommended; he was obviously experienced, and he radiated confidence. He said he'd done hundreds of these operations. The only time there was a problem was due to a blood clot.

I hadn't been paying much attention to his spiel up to that point, but I did right then. I noticed how his face had become suddenly grave. He informed me that he'd recently lost a patient due to an embolism caused by postsurgical deep vein thrombosis. Translation: his patient died due to a heart attack caused by a blood clot of the vein carrying blood to the liver. For some reason, if there were a blood clot, he would not be able to go in and operate again. Furthermore, in such circumstances, chances of survival were slim.

He emphasized that the chances of me getting a blood clot were almost zero, especially at my age (I was in my late thirties at the time). Nevertheless, he wasn't about to take any chances; so, right after the surgery, he told me I'd be having a 3D ultrasound. This was nonnegotiable if I wanted him as my surgeon. He was concerned, because most insurance companies asserted that surgery was not adequate reason to justify such an extremely costly exam, and I might have to incur the cost myself. I didn't mind. I wanted to have the surgery, and I wanted the best surgeon doing it. I needed this disease gone from my life. I had been sick for most of the year and if this surgery didn't fix things, I'd be looking at permanent disability and a shortened life span due to all the drugs I'd have to take to control the hemolytic anemia.

And now here I was, the very next day after the surgery, with a blood clot.

There was no question that I had a blood clot. The sonographer had said so and there was no way she was wrong; she'd had four doctors confirm the diagnosis.

A postsurgical blood clot meant death.

The question was one of time.

I had the right to know if it was a matter of minutes, hours, or days. I knew it couldn't be much longer than that.

But not one passerby would speak to me.

I don't recall ever being afraid in a hospital or a doctor's office, but for some reason, that day, I was in a state of silent hysteria. It might have had something to do with the rapid tapering off of high dosages of prednisone prior to surgery.

I was alone. Temporarily abandoned. These might be the very last moments of my life. There I was, in this ugly, colorless corridor, with that depressing fluorescent light pounding down on my eyes.

Any other time, I would have gotten up and walked away. But I'd just had surgery and I was on painkillers. I was immobilized physically and paralyzed psychologically.

There wasn't even a clock to look at, and I wasn't wearing a watch either. They had taken all those things from me when I'd gone in for surgery. I'd get them back. Sure. If I were alive to receive them, that is.

My mother was out there, somewhere, waiting. If only she knew.

My wife was in Greece. So was my son. They knew about the surgery, but I hadn't told them about the blood-clot risk. Why worry them when the chances were minuscule? This is why: because I was the one-in-ten-thousand statistic with a post-op blood clot, and it was going to end my life.

No chance to even say goodbye.

Anger welled up in me, but the adrenaline wasn't enough to get me moving out of that mobile hospital bed.

I had the right to know.

I had the right.

But what use were my rights when I had no means to enforce them?

I tried to think of a solution. Something I could actually do, other than worrying. But I couldn't come up with anything.

So I followed my thoughts to the dark places they took me and suffered until a PEA (patient escort aide—what used to be called an orderly) finally wheeled me to my room.

An hour later, I got to speak with my surgeon.

I wasn't going to die after all. Yes, I had a clot, but by some insane coincidence it had nothing to do with the surgery—it had to do with living in Arizona and having been dehydrated at some point. Amazing because it was in the hepatic portal vein—precisely where it would have been had this been a postoperative blood clot.

The odds of discovering a blood clot in exactly the same place as where the postoperative blood clot would have been were too absurd to even put into numbers.

Though I may have had what would be considered legitimate cause to worry, the negative, destructive thoughts that I was believing while I was in the corridor offered nothing whatsoever in terms of value (practical or psychological).

I'd been immobilized—there was nothing I could do, nobody who could answer my questions, nobody to even talk to, and I didn't even have a way of keeping track of time.

I was stuck, alone with my thoughts.

Back then, I did not have the ITTIL technique to rely on, and therefore I had no choice but to believe and identify with my thoughts.

That served to elevate my fear and my anger at the situation. A situation I believed was completely unfair—spending what I imagined could be the last moments of my life in a grim hospital corridor, imprisoned with my thoughts.

If I'd had the ITTIL technique at the time, those thoughts would have been seen as untrue. I would have also seen, in that situation, none of those thoughts were beneficial either. Seen as untrue and not beneficial they would have been easy to drop.

There is no way to know what other thoughts would have arisen in that situation had I used the ITTIL technique, just as there's no way to know what thoughts will arise in the next thirty seconds (ITTIL technique or not). What I do know is that with the ITTIL technique, I would have been at peace, because no thought would have been seen as true and I'd be using only the thoughts that had value to me.

There would have been no belief, therefore there would have been no suffering.

WHEN THOUGHT IS MADE INTO A PROBLEM

Thoughts arise all the time. We have no control over them, and neither do we have control over what thoughts they are. During the waking state, thoughts typically arise in the form of an unending commentary, constantly comparing, evaluating, judging. We compare with the past or an imagined future. In this way, thoughts, when believed, continually resist the present moment.

For most people, most thoughts are negative, and occasionally downright destructive in nature.

Research in psychology has shown that negative chatter in the brain (negative recurring thoughts) comprises 60 to 70 percent of thought, a phenomenon referred to as negative dominance. [1]

People believe that truth is out there and that it can be understood at the level of thinking. The common belief is that it's just a matter of gaining knowledge of truth by means of discovery. It is further believed that one can use this knowledge, this thought-gained truth, as a means to explain the past and control the future. Since people believe situations cause their suffering, if truth can control events, it can also control their suffering.

A more fundamental reason, however, is that most people believe they *are* their thoughts. This creates a deep identification with thought, and so to believe in a thought is to believe in oneself, in one's very identity.

Thoughts can serve as a great tool. Extraordinary advances in science and technology are a testimony to this. In addition to identifying with our thoughts and believing that thoughts can offer truth, there's also a tendency to confuse value with validity. In other words, if a thought serves us, we tend to believe it without question.

Thoughts are only ever a problem when people identify with and believe them.

Without the element of belief, there are no good or bad thoughts; there are only beneficial thoughts in the moment.

THOUGHTS, BELIEFS, AND SUFFERING

We Think, We Believe, and We Suffer

Thoughts arise, and since most of us identify with our thoughts and believe them unquestioningly, as a result, we suffer.

---

1 See *Psychology Today:* How Negative Is Your "Mental Chatter"? https:// www.psychologytoday.com/blog/sapient-nature/201310/how-negative-is -your-mental-chatter.

Let's take a quick peek, breaking down the process as it occurs.

WE THINK

Thoughts arise. Most of us believe we have control over them. In our experience, however, we have as much control over thoughts as we do the movement or number of clouds in the sky. If we did have control, we would know what we'd be thinking a minute from now.

WE BELIEVE

Most of us believe pretty much every thought that pops up.

The fundamental belief that is at the core of our compulsion to believe is that we *are* our thoughts. And so if we are to believe in ourselves, we must believe our thoughts.

We are conditioned to believe that it is possible to have intellectual knowledge of truth. We believe that there is truth that can be attained by thought—it's just a matter of somehow discovering this truth.

We also tend to confuse value with validity. In other words, if a thought serves us, repeatedly and consistently, we tend to consider it truer (possibly even going so far as to label it a fact) than a thought that is rarely of value.

Many people believe that it is impossible to function without belief.

We've all heard the expression "I find that hard to believe." The implication here is that people actually *try* to believe things, and sometimes fail. It seems we are conditioned this way.

We have a thought, we identify with it (it's who we think we are, after all), and then work to confirm our belief in the thought by use of reason. In other words, we support a belief in a thought with other thoughts we believe.

When a thought arises, we follow that thought to wherever it leads us. Most people rarely question the validity of their thoughts; they simply believe them.

There's another reason why we believe our thoughts indiscriminately. Seemingly more-objective thoughts (thoughts that are considered true by most people) are mixed in with obviously subjective thoughts (thoughts that you have but others may or may not agree with), and so *all thoughts, regardless of their nature, are generally believed to be true.* Therefore, an apparently objective thought that says the table is solid and brown could be blended in with a clearly subjective thought that says the table looks ugly, it doesn't match the rest of the furniture, and the owner obviously has no taste whatsoever.

Let's say you observe someone losing a tennis match to a player you are about to challenge for first place. The person who lost is your friend, and you consider him one of the toughest opponents you have ever faced.

You perceive what you believe is an external reality. This perception comes through constructs and labels. You see colors, and these are made into shapes and forms that you immediately identify: tennis court, scoreboard, people. These object labels are considered less subjective thoughts. Then you identify people: friend, his opponent (soon to be your opponent).

You perceive the colors that you shape into and identify as a scoreboard.

You identify the numbers six and two. Six represents the opponent. The final score declares the winner and the loser. Your math is verified on the megaphone and by the behavior of the two players.

Your friend lost. He is on the court, knees to the ground like he's praying. His opponent is jumping up and down, his racket raised in victory. This is all processed very quickly. These would be the so-called objective thoughts. Your turn is coming soon. Another relatively objective thought.

You don't believe you can do better than your friend. That is a more-subjective thought. You're probably going to lose. Another subjective thought. You might have a chance if you deliver fast top spins to your opponent's backhand. He'll figure out your strategy and counter with short balls to the net. Subjective thoughts.

If you lose this game, you're out of the tournament and all those intense workouts, all the sacrifices you made, will be for nothing.

You're already sweating now, and the match hasn't even begun.

What happened here?

You believed the thoughts that parsed the colors into shapes into a tennis court without question.

The same applies to the thoughts that identified your friend and his opponent.

You believed the numbers as well. You saw the players' behaviors, and they confirmed your belief about who'd won and who'd lost.

You also believed that you'd probably lose. This thought rides along with the other more "objective" thoughts, and so you believed them all without taking the time to discriminate between two different types of thoughts.

All these thoughts went off like a string of firecrackers. They were grouped together, the net reeled in, and you believed them all— hook, line, and sinker.

The normal experience of thoughts is to believe them all, without discernment, and regardless of their degree of subjectivity.

WE SUFFER

Because it is vital that we see why belief must be eliminated altogether in order for suffering to be eliminated, we must acquire an understanding of how belief causes suffering. I go into this topic in depth, and with examples, in the very next chapter.

When you believe, you are encaged by that belief, and see everything in the moment from that perspective. As a result, you're not open to whatever arises in the moment. This conflict with the present situation, this resistance, is suffering. Since you identify with your beliefs, when whatever happens doesn't coincide with what you believe should be happening, you are torn. Furthermore, belief breeds doubt because for every belief there is an opposing belief. Doubt creates internal conflict. It attacks the original belief by using the reasoning that supports the opposing belief. Because we identify with our beliefs, we either defend them by trying to find better reasoning to conquer our doubt, we modify them in an attempt to outmaneuver our doubt, or we change them altogether.

Where there's internal conflict, there's usually external conflict. That external conflict is created in the clash between people who hold opposing beliefs.

So for most of us, we think, we believe, and as a result, we suffer.

USING THOUGHTS RATHER THAN BEING USED BY THOUGHTS

The ITTIL technique does two things: first and foremost, it eliminates one's belief in a thought. Once that happens, the thought is then used as a tool rather than as a source of truth. Viewed as a tool, a thought has the potential to be beneficial, with no downside (suffering).

Instead of using thoughts as evidence to support your belief, or doing the opposite—trying to suppress a thought with drugs, other addictive behaviors, or entertainment, the ITTIL technique eliminates the source of the suffering by removing the main cause—belief.

To use thoughts without belief is to free yourself from the self-torture that occurs when you believe a thought.

Without belief, thinking becomes more focused. Circular, recurring thoughts eventually go away because they have no value, and there's nothing for them to prove since, without belief, nothing needs proving. There is no doubt, because there is no belief to be contradicted and thereby generate doubt.

Without belief, there is the freedom to use thoughts while at the same time being completely free from attachment to thought.

Some people believe that it is impossible to function without belief. Rather than simply saying that statement is untrue, I'll go one step further and suggest that once you learn how, you apply the ITTIL technique and see for yourself: not only is it possible to function without belief but in doing so, you will be clear, focused, and most important, free of suffering.

Thoughts become something akin to tools in a toolbox. Sometimes they're beneficial sometimes they're not, but if used at the right time, and if used properly (without the element of belief) they have the potential of being of great benefit.

The ITTIL technique eliminates belief in thought. When thoughts are treated as tools at your service, you no longer risk becoming a tool at the service of your thoughts.

The ITTIL technique is a completely open approach to thinking, and it allows for any thought to arise without opposing it, suppressing it, ignoring it, or restricting it to only something positive (for example, positive affirmation).

Negative, useless thinking comes to an end, as does the need to dull your thinking with drugs, alcohol, or other addictive behaviors.

Instead, with the ITTIL technique, all thoughts are seen as equally untrue and become potentially beneficial tools in the moment.

HOW THE ITTIL TECHNIQUE
BREAKS DOWN THOUGHTS

The ITTIL technique is a practice, not a philosophy.

However, through the practice of the ITTIL technique, in the process of eliminating belief one thought at a time, you will no longer identify yourself with your thoughts and it will eventually become evident that even the statement philosopher René Descartes considered to be beyond doubt, "I think, therefore I am," is not true. Thoughts come to be seen as tools, not as truths. They are either beneficial at the time they arise, or not.

Your left hand, for example, is clearly not what you are. If you lose your left hand, there isn't less of *you*. You don't use your left hand at every moment—it is a tool available to you the moment it is seen as useful. Paying the cashier, you might need change from your right pocket. You would likely find your right hand more useful. Moments later, as you approach your car, in trying to fish out your keys from your left pocket, you would probably decide that your left hand is useful at that particular moment.

Similarly, when a thought arises, the ITTIL technique eliminates the element of belief and simply evaluates whether the thought is beneficial at this particular moment.

With belief out of the equation, thoughts are no longer seen as good or bad, only as beneficial in the moment or not.

Thoughts That Cause Noticeable Suffering

In the beginning, only thoughts that trigger any form of noticeable suffering are addressed. This suffering can range in intensity from boredom, restlessness, and irritability, to anger, fear, anxiety, sadness, depression, shame, and guilt.

- "I'm too fat."
- "I just made a terrible mistake."
- "My job is sucking the life out of me."
- "I shouldn't have gotten out of bed today."
- "I hate Monday-night football."

In advanced applications, the ITTIL technique is used on any thought believed to be true.

- "My name is _____ ."
- "I'm _____ years old."
- "I was born in _____ ."
- "It is cold outside."
- "It is raining outside."
- "The universe was the result of an explosion of a singularity."

Questioning Thoughts

The ITTIL technique is meant to be applied on statements only, not on questions.

In order to use the ITTIL technique on all thoughts, however, even questions have to be addressed. To do so, thoughts that appear as questions must be converted into statements, thereby exposing the beliefs and assumptions implicit in the question itself. (More on this in chapter 5.)

Here's an example.

- "Am I a total loser for being unsuccessful?"

Let's break down the first part of this question into a statement:

- "I am a loser."

The assumed truth is that the thinker is a loser.

Furthermore, "I am a *total* loser" assumes that there is some scale to being a loser.

Now let's break down the last part of this question:

- The assumption is that the thinker is unsuccessful.

Here is a more involved example:

- "What happens when you die?"

The assumptions are that:

1. Something happens when you die.
2. You will die.
3. There is a "you" that can therefore die.

All Thoughts

The ITTIL technique serves to eliminate belief and the suffering it causes, awakening you in the moment to what is. Since all belief must be eliminated for all suffering to end, no thought is exempt, even thoughts that arise in the form of a question. However, questioning thoughts and seemingly more-objective thoughts are best left for advanced applications of the technique.

DISTINGUISHING BETWEEN PRACTICAL AND PSYCHOLOGICAL THOUGHTS

It became obvious to me early on that in order to better explain some of the fundamental principles and applications of the ITTIL technique, it was necessary to differentiate between what might be conventionally characterized objective thoughts and thoughts that are seemingly more subjective.

Another goal of identifying various types of thoughts is to purge the conventional narrative that says that some thoughts are truer than others.

Using the terms "objective" and "subjective" when differentiating between types of thoughts doesn't work, simply because there is no such thing as an objective thought—all thoughts are subjective. Furthermore, to label a thought as objective would assume a scale of validity, or truth value, and would therefore go against the fundamental premise of the ITTIL technique which is that all thoughts are equally untrue.

Using quotation marks around the word "objective" or continually prefacing the word with "apparently" or "seemingly" would be tiring and potentially confusing.

The best solution I could come up with was to use "practical" and "psychological" as adjectives to categorize the two kinds of thoughts.

I'm not sure how a psychologist would define a psychological thought or if they would do so at all. It might be that all thoughts are considered psychological. But for the purposes of this book, and for gauging the technique from easier to more-advanced applications, it is necessary to make a simple, if simplistic, distinction between the two.

As with all the definitions given in this book, they are not necessarily "dictionary correct," but they are beneficial, and that's all they need to be for ITTIL to work its magic.

Practical thought is any thought that may be considered by *conventional reasoning* to be logical, *reasonably* objective, and have some practical application not only to the thinker but to others for whom the thought has occurred or to whom it has been communicated.

Examples:

- "That is a chair."
- "Angela is twenty."

Psychological thought, on the other hand, is any thought that may be considered by conventional reasoning to be highly subjective.

Examples:

- "That's one butt-ugly chair."
- "Angela is totally hot."

It is important to remember that for the purposes of the ITTIL technique, neither the thought, "That is a chair," nor the thought, "That is one butt-ugly chair," is true.

Both are equally untrue.

The same goes for "Angela is twenty," and "Angela is totally hot."

PSYCHOLOGICAL THOUGHTS AND THE ITTIL TECHNIQUE

When we believe our psychological thoughts, the suffering that occurs is very clear and apparent, as is the relief from this suffering that results when dropping belief in the psychological thought.

If I'm believing a thought that says, "I just made a terrible mistake," I might experience anxiety, guilt, or possibly even fear.

When I no longer believe that thought, the associated suffering is lifted.

In such cases, the effect and power of belief is readily apparent.

There are times, especially when it comes to psychological thoughts, when the underlying thought is not obvious.

The "I AM THINKING . . ." companion technique (see chapter 5) is used for those times when the negative impact of a belief—the resulting suffering—is self-evident, but the thought behind it remains elusive.

It can also be used on thoughts that are highly subtle in nature. Such thoughts may come in the form of images or they might simply arise as a "sense" of something. These thoughts are converted to concrete statements so that the ITTIL technique can be applied.

FULFILLMENT ACTIONS FOR PSYCHOLOGICAL THOUGHTS

Psychological thoughts are those that are clearly associated with some emotion or feeling. In the beginning, we apply the ITTIL technique only on what are considered negative feelings. There is no philosophy required to see how these negative feelings constitute an expression of some degree of suffering.

Feel the Emotion and Find the Psychological Thought

The first step in this fulfillment action is to sit quietly and recall a time when you were having an intense negative emotion. Visualize the situation.

We want to start with intense negative emotions, because finding the thought behind these feelings is typically a lot easier than uncovering a thought that is making you feel slightly restless or uncomfortable.

For instance, if the feeling is intense anger, go back in your imagination and try to re-create that anger. Find the thought that really makes you boil just the way it did back when you experienced that feeling. Find the thought that kept you up most of the night.

Maybe you just got home and realized the guy who left for Las Vegas sold you a car that was a lemon. The thought would be, "He sold me a lemon."

All that is needed at this point is to find the statement that, when repeated to yourself, makes you feel as close as possible to how you were feeling back then.

It is important to note that the past might be just several seconds ago. When you are finding the thought that you are believing, you are always looking at a past thought.

Uprooting an Underlying Psychological Thought

Finding a thought that is the core psychological thought behind your negative feeling right off the bat doesn't happen every single time.

More often than not, it will take several attempts to get the thought just right so that you are feeling the full intensity of the negative emotion.

In the fulfillment actions from the end of chapter 1, we saw how modifying the original statement slightly by changing a few words could help identify the thought that resonates most.

For this fulfillment action, allow this to occur on its own.

Simply maintain your attention on the negative feeling, and look at what thoughts arise. With each thought, preface it with the words "I AM THINKING . . ."

So, going back to the example about the car: "I AM THINKING . . . the guy sold me a lemon."

Let's say that thought is close, but you're not really as livid as you were when it happened.

So you keep your attention on the feeling and allow the next thought. "I AM THINKING . . . I let myself get suckered again."

And again: "I AM THINKING . . . when I trust people, they betray me."

If at this point, you're seeing red—just as you did when the situation arose, you have your statement and you're then ready to apply the ITTIL technique (see chapter 5).

PRACTICAL THOUGHTS AND THE ITTIL TECHNIQUE

The application of the ITTIL technique is exactly the same no matter whether it's a psychological or practical thought.

The ITTIL technique is applied to statements, and so all questions, whether they are made up of psychological or practical assumptions, must first be broken up into statements. (We have seen how this is done earlier in this chapter. Detailed examples are also given in chapter 5.)

However, at first, only negative psychological thoughts—thoughts that cause some degree of identifiable suffering are addressed. Practical thoughts are left for advanced applications of the ITTIL technique (see chapter 6), because the underlying effects of the suffering associated with belief in practical thoughts are far more subtle (though not less powerful) than with psychological thoughts. Also, the process of reasoning required to invalidate practical thoughts is more involved.

The following are clearly practical questions and would need to be converted into statements:

- "Is that a brown chair?"
- "What color is that car?"
- "How many trees are there in my backyard?"

These are the derived practical statements:

- "That is a brown chair."
- "This is a blue car."
- "There are four trees in my backyard."

FULFILLMENT ACTION FOR PRACTICAL THOUGHTS

Distinguishing Practical Thoughts

Sit quietly and write down your thoughts as they arise.

Write down ten unrelated thoughts. Don't hold on to or follow your thoughts; that way it won't take long before ten unrelated thoughts arise. If a thought is related to one already written down, wait for the next one until you have written down ten unrelated thoughts.

Repeat each thought to yourself and look for the slightest signs of a reaction in yourself, even if it's a barely detectible restlessness. Mark these thoughts as psychological thoughts. If there isn't the slighted noticeable discomfort, then mark the thought as a practical thought.

Note the proportion of psychological thoughts to practical ones.

After utilizing the ITTIL technique for a while, the number of psychological thoughts you have will be dramatically reduced.

3.
What Lies in Belief

A SPECIAL STORY

For most of my life, I believed I was special.

This was so obvious that it never even occurred to me to question this belief.

Though I wouldn't admit it out loud or, on some level, even to myself, I also believed that my being special was the reason people loved me.

I was my father's son. Right there, I believed that meant I was special, at least to him. There was only one other person on this planet that could say the same, and that person was my brother. Therefore, I was at least as special as he was.

But that wasn't enough, of course. If being special meant people loved me, then I was determined to be as special as possible. I tried to excel in piano, karate, chess, and table tennis. At seventeen, I'd lived in four different countries, spoke three languages, and was in the process of learning another two. I was a year ahead of my peers at one of the best high schools in the world and was hoping to get into an Ivy League college. I'd also tried souping up my moped to make it the fastest in the country, but that one was on me—I didn't believe anybody else would really care. (If I'd wanted to be really cool, I'd wait until I was eighteen and ride a motorcycle.)

I was in Greece when it happened.

My father and I were in the middle of a major argument. It was the only real argument I remember ever having with him. I was in awe of my father, and a little afraid of him as well. How I got myself in the position of arguing with my father, I do not recall. I think it had something to do with keeping the relapse of my ulcerative colitis a secret. He'd found a bloodstain on the coattails of one of my shirts. There may have been a scolding on his part, or it may have been what started the argument, I don't remember. Actually, I don't remember a single word that I said to him. I just remember something he said to me. Something that stuck with me my entire life.

We were in a narrow corridor of his house. The only way out was past him. He said, "You think you're special, young man, but you're not."

I'd dismissed his words at the time, rationalizing that he was angry and he hadn't meant it. I'd stood up to him, and I'd never done that before, so I figured he'd retaliated with a blow below the belt.

Angry or not, those words came back to haunt me over the years. What did he mean by that?

If I wasn't special, then that meant he didn't love me, and I knew that wasn't true. I knew he loved me. So how could he love me if I wasn't special? I was caught in a loop.

Just being his son made me special. That was enough for most dads to love their kids, wasn't it? Plus I had all these other things going for me, so why on earth would he say I wasn't special? Even if I'd been a thief and a drug addict, I'd still be special, right? Maybe not in a good way, but still special.

Doubt set in, with an opposing rationale: some things said in anger are things that people believe but don't dare say in other situations. Similar to teasing or words said in jest. An argument serves as an excuse to say what you really feel.

Of all people, I believed my father knew more than anyone else how special I was, until that fight.

To be fair, he'd never told me I was special. I'd just assumed he thought so because as far as I was concerned my specialness was a given as much as was the air I breathed.

And since I believed that my father's love for me had to be on account of the fact that I was special, instead of seeing the possibility that I was worthy of love whether I was special or not, I questioned whether I was loved at all, because my belief that I had to be special in order to be loved was so deeply rooted.

I spent decades trying to maintain my special qualities. I kept striving for and achieving higher and higher goals. I was never satisfied, though, because I continued to believe that love was dependent on my differentiating myself from others.

After I began using the ITTIL technique, I dropped the belief that I was special.

It was shortly after my father's death that I recalled the argument I'd had with him decades earlier. In it I saw the revelation in his words. Whether he'd intended his statement as a means to chastise and subdue me in order to win the argument, or whether his words came from a deep understanding of human nature, I don't know. And it didn't matter.

From my post-ITTIL perspective, his words were wonderfully freeing. All of the things that make someone special are transitory and therefore not true. When I'm in deep sleep, I still am what I am, and what is there in my direct experience then that is special? I have nothing to compare with, so I cannot be special. Also, I can only be special relative to someone else. Therefore, again, the idea that I'm special isn't true. I also saw that I'm not special in not being special. In other words, if I'm not special, no one is special.

I don't need to be special in any way to be loved. Now there's nothing I need do. I don't need to prove myself worthy of love. That said, I still do things that the old me might have considered as making me special. The difference is that now I do them out of enthusiasm and love for what I'm doing, not out of any desire to be special so that I can be loved.

It's amazing to me now to observe how this simple yet fundamental belief set the course of my life for almost half a century.

THE COMMON VIEW
OF BELIEF AND FAITH

In the story about my argument with my father, there is little chance of confusing what was clearly a belief for me with faith. This is one of the reasons I chose that story.

However, for many, belief is a kind of synonym for faith.

- "I believe in you."
- "I have faith in you."

Both of the above statements would typically be viewed as one and the same.

According to an article, "Religion and Belief," from the Council of Europe, "Belief is a state of the mind when we consider something true even though we are not 100% sure or able to prove it." [2]

The Merriam-Webster dictionary, meanwhile, defines belief as follows:

1   : a state or habit of mind in which trust or confidence is placed in some person or thing • her *belief* in God • a *belief* in democracy • I bought the table in the *belief* that it was an antique • contrary to popular *belief*

2   : something that is accepted, considered to be true, or held as an opinion : something believed • an individual's

---

[2] Council of Europe, "Religion and Belief," https://www.coe.int/en/web /compass/religion-and-belief, accessed March 7, 2018.

religious or political *beliefs*; especially : a tenet or body of tenets held by a group • the *beliefs* of the Catholic Church

3   : conviction of the truth of some statement or the reality of some being or phenomenon especially when based on examination of evidence • *belief* in the validity of scientific statements [3]

Dictionary.com, on the other hand, defines belief as "confidence; faith; trust," and as "a religious tenet or tenets; religious creed or faith." [4]

For the purposes of this book, it is essential that there is a clear understanding of the manner in which the word *belief* is used.

THE ITTIL DISTINCTION BETWEEN BELIEF AND FAITH

The ITTIL perspective defines *faith* and *belief* as follows:

> *Faith transcends thought and is not based on reasoning. If reasoning is used to support faith, then by definition, it isn't faith, it's a belief.*

Faith is defined here so as to contrast and distinguish it clearly from belief.

For the purposes of ITTIL, belief and faith are entirely different things.

Belief is born of thought.

Faith lies outside the realm of thought.

---

[3] https://www.merriam-webster.com/dictionary/belief
[4] http://www.dictionary.com/browse/belief

Belief is a conviction based on thought. Something is believed to be true through a process of reasoning (thinking).

Faith is an assertion of something being true without proof. For the purposes of this book, and as defined by ITTIL, faith, like love, transcends thought.

Again, I am well aware that others have different definitions of belief and faith. For some, faith is but a stronger, deeper form of belief. And for others, a belief can arise without reasoning.

It is crucial that the definition of belief be understood completely in order for ITTIL to have beneficial results.

I mention faith to clearly distinguish it from belief, since the two are often confused.

While faith is not required for the practice of ITTIL, it is entirely possible to have faith and still use ITTIL.

Belief, on the other hand, has no place in ITTIL. In fact, eradicating any and all belief is essential to and is the foundation of ITTIL.

We are not our thoughts, despite the common belief to the contrary.

There is a state of deep sleep, a state of transcendence, a comatose state, a state we go into when under general anesthesia. The very brief moments between thoughts. When these states occur, we do not cease to exist. Because if we did, then somehow we would be coming in and out of existence fairly often. Therefore there is a place for faith to exist other than in the realm of thought.

Belief, on the other hand—again, as defined here—is based on reason. I believe this or that *because* . . .

In the case of the argument with my father, I believed I was special. It was a belief because it was founded on reasoning. I was special *because* . . . I was his son; *because* I'd accumulated a host of accomplishments that distinguished me from others.

I did not have *faith* that I was special. Direct experience, looking at what I am, would not have shown that I was special, and so it wasn't faith. Even back then, I wouldn't have used the word faith for my specialness.

I would have used faith regarding my father's love for me, however. That didn't require reasoning. Even when he was angry at me, even when he was saying I wasn't special, there was no question that he loved me. I had faith in the love he had for me.

Today I can say I have faith in faith. I can also say I have faith in love. Both faith and love, however, exist outside the realm of thought and therefore of reason.

If you have faith (or faith has you, depending on your perspective), the good news is that your faith is *not* affected in *any way* by ITTIL, as long as it remains faith, and not belief.

To most, the question "Why do you love your child?" is simply absurd. You don't need to explain it; you love your child unquestioningly. It isn't something that you have reasoned into being. It isn't a belief. Like faith, you simply love, and that love is outside the domain of thought. I don't think my father would have offered any explanation for his love for me, just as I have none for my love for my children. I simply love. There's no question about it; it's beyond explanation, and yet it's more real than the keyboard I'm typing on.

I have been asked why I love my wife, and I can see why this question might arise. Some people define love differently. They see it as a cause-and-effect thing. According to my definition, however, if I have to explain it, if there's a "because," then it isn't love, it's some thought that is about love.

This applies to faith as well.

If there's a "because," then it isn't faith, it's a belief—a thought about faith.

Faith is complete surrender at a level beyond thought.

THE ITTIL DEFINITION OF BELIEF

Belief is based on, held together, and maintained
by reasoning. In other words, by thought.

It is essential that the definition of belief and the distinction of it from faith be crystal clear. Time and time again, I have seen that without this distinction, confusion and resistance often arise, especially when introducing the ITTIL technique to religious people.

For the purposes of ITTIL:

Belief is an assertion that something is true through a process of reasoning. Put another way, belief is conviction based on thought.

Faith is an assertion that something is true without proof.

In other words, if reasoning is being used to establish or maintain faith, then by definition it is not faith, it is belief.

Definitions of belief, as with most definitions, can vary from person to person.

However, whenever the word *belief* appears in this book, it refers to an assertion that something is true through a process of reasoning and has no association with faith whatsoever.

THE COMPULSION TO BELIEVE

If we believe the thought that says, "I think, therefore I am," then our very existence is defined by our thought. The compulsion to believe our thoughts stems from this fundamental belief that claims we actually *are* our thoughts.

For most of us, a state of no thought is a state akin to death. When people suffer from extreme dementia and cannot even maintain basic bodily functions, they are often cruelly referred to as vegetables. Or "as good as dead."

"That's not my *real* grandmother," people will say, or, "That's not the grandmother I once knew."

The compulsion to believe also arises because we believe there is truth out there. We are so certain about some "facts," we believe there is no question whether truth can be known by thought. Of course it can, we say. Therefore since it is believed that thought can divine truth, the compulsion to believe is not only justified, it is encouraged.

If a thought is accepted by almost everyone as being unquestionably true, then if one thing can be true, there can be more than one truth.

Here's an example: Angela is standing on a bus, and the bus is solid.

Who would question that? Very few people. It's a practical thought, so why question it? Why question the validity of something with such obvious utility? Because accepting even the most practical and seemingly factual thought as true opens a Pandora's box wherein not only are there many truths, there are infinite degrees of truth. This is the way most people have been thinking for centuries, and it has led to the compulsion to believe and the resulting suffering that has made up much of the history of humankind.

And though under this conventional paradigm, most of us believe there are degrees of truth, more often than not our compulsion to believe leads us to accept all our thoughts and believe them indiscriminately, regardless of the assumed degree to which each thought is considered true—and despite whether they are practical or psychological in nature.

The undesirable effects of the compulsion to believe a negative psychological thought is obvious: it's not beneficial and it is even potentially harmful.

But what about practical thoughts? How can believing those thoughts lead to suffering? In other words, where's the problem in accepting thoughts as truth and pursuing truth in thoughts?

The problem is that *when thoughts come together in a quick stream, the intensity of belief that commonly accompanies practical thoughts tends to bleed over into the psychological thoughts that come in the mix.*

To see how this works, I'll give a simple example of both practical and psychological thoughts and the dynamic that results when the compulsion toward belief is involved.

Example: *It's Angela's thirty-third birthday and she's on the bus on her way to court to try to get her payback from the scoundrel who deceived her for ten years, stealing her hard-earned money and ruining her business in the process. It's raining, and it isn't hard to guess what she's concealing behind those sunglasses other than tears.*

We are conditioned to accept statements as facts.

If there were time to process these statements and sort them out relative to their degrees of truth, we'd have something like this:

> Fact: It is raining.
> Fact: Angela is on a bus.
> Fact: Angela is wearing sunglasses.
> Fact: Tears are dripping from behind Angela's
>   sunglasses.
> Fact: Angela is thirty-three and it is her birthday.
> Highly likely: She's going to court.
> Highly likely: She has a bruised eye.
> Probable: She was beaten by the same man who
>   deceived her and stole from her for ten years.

The facts in the list are accepted without question.

We accept that she's going to court, but since it hasn't yet happened, we can't be certain. Because it is raining, we assume it is also dark. Therefore she's wearing the shades so people won't see her bruised eye. She's crying, and this bolsters the hypothesis that she's been beaten. The man she's going to confront in court is a scoundrel who has deceived her for ten years, stealing her hard-earned money and ruining her business in the process. This is where our focus is, and we're not sure about the whole story. Her bruised eye and her tears and the fact that she's going to court all support this story. But there has to be more to it. There are things we don't know. Our attention is on these things, because we're on her side and we want to see her win. We've identified with her and so we want her suffering to end.

We have been trained to accept certain things as facts. As undeniable truths. This means that we can know truth using reasoning. Using our thoughts. This belief creates a desire to find truth in order to control the future and explain the past. In order to find truth using reasoning (thought), the thoughts must be based on some truth to begin with. And so we lie to ourselves, pretending that we know some truth in order to discover more truth. Once more truth is discovered, it is added to the reservoir of beliefs that we hold. The compulsion to believe creates a false security and keeps us from questioning the truths we have already accepted.

In the example just related, we *believe* in order to explain the past and find out the entire truth about what happened to Angela, and to control the future by using the facts we have learned to protect her.

We believe that it is dark, for instance, when the rain could have been a sun shower. The sunglasses could have been to protect from the glare. For all we know, she could have been laughing herself to tears thinking about how she was going to get back at the guy in court. We believe she was crying, but was she? All we know that was listed as a fact was that tears appeared from behind her sunglasses. We didn't have much time to examine our thoughts, of course, and most of us aren't like Sherlock Holmes or Mr. Spock. But even Mr. Holmes would have considered it a fact that she was on a bus, that it was raining, that it was her birthday, and that she was thirty-three. Because Mr. Holmes would believe in facts. He'd believe that truth can be known by reasoning and therefore by thoughts.

The belief that thoughts can divine truth is based on a prior belief that there is no other way to function. This belief that we must believe in order to function creates the compulsion to believe.

This belief is not true, the compulsion keeps us from questioning it. This compulsion to believe keeps us perpetually in the dark as we lock ourselves in the thought trap of using lies to find truth.

Since we were toddlers, we've internalized the compulsion to believe in believing itself. *We have ascertained that there is truth out there to be discovered by thought.* We have been taught lies, and we have assigned ourselves the impossible task of finding truth using these lies.

In the example given, someone practicing ITTIL would see all the listed statements as equally untrue (this will be explained in chapter 4—What Lies in Truth) and would find the opposing statements to the ones that were listed.

- Angela is on a bus. Angela is *not* on a bus.
- Angela is wearing sunglasses. Angela is *not* wearing sunglasses.
- Angela is crying. Angela is *not* crying.
- Angela is thirty-three. Angela is *not* thirty-three.
- She's going to court. She's *not* going to court.
- She has a bruised eye. She *doesn't* have a bruised eye.

Each statement and its opposite are untrue.

Many of these statements could be useful. Without a compulsion to believe, you are free to use the statements and not be attached to them. There is no truth there to rattle you—to tear you apart, to hurt you. There are only useful statements in the moment. Again, more on that later. Suffice it to say, to be free of belief is to be free of suffering and completely open to all possibilities. As such, were you driven to do so, you'd be in the best position to offer Angela help.

The compulsion to believe also arises because of the generally accepted wisdom that beliefs are not only necessary in order to function, they are helpful.

We believe this to be especially true in respect to positive thoughts.

There is a tendency, and even a movement, to believe positive thoughts. This is because belief in positive thoughts often leads to positive feelings.

However, maintaining those positive feelings is not possible, because they are based on thoughts, and thoughts are fleeting.

Thoughts come and go, and we don't have control over what thoughts arise. Positive affirmation entails focusing on positive thoughts, encouraging them, believing them, while at the same time swatting away the negative ones. This practice always fails, because belief generates doubt. There will always be opposing reasoning to dismantle the positive belief.

One argument that encourages the compulsion to believe positive thoughts is that if it isn't working, it's because you're not doing it right!

This is not true, however, because where there is belief, be it in something positive or negative, there is always suffering.

Each thought construct in which we believe forms a string that becomes a story. We carry veritable libraries of fiction with us and can no longer see or hear or smell without creating some story that we then believe and we call reality.

Whether the story is a fairy tale with a happy ending or the most terrifying nightmare, the result is always suffering, because we are caught up in the story and unable to escape for as long as we use beliefs to perpetuate fiction.

The compulsion to believe is a compulsion to control. That compulsion leads to suffering because belief has control over nothing.

Belief perpetually resists, and that isn't control, that is pain.

How belief causes suffering is the topic of the next section.

BELIEF LEADS TO SUFFERING

Eliminating belief is at the core of the ITTIL technique, and so it is vital to understand how belief causes suffering.

As promised in chapter 2, this section offers an in-depth look at these reasons and the following section provides examples for each.

Belief breeds conflict, both internal and external, and conflict is suffering.

Internal conflict expresses itself as anger, fear, anxiety, sadness, depression, shame, guilt, and the whole range of negative emotions.

External conflict expresses itself as violence. There are two expressions of violence: nonphysical violence in the form of body language and written or spoken words, and physical violence ranging from an unloving poke to outright war and the whole gamut in between.

Belief Brings Internal Conflict

This internal conflict arises in two forms:

1. **Conflict between your belief and the present situation**

   • When you believe, you are encaged by that belief, and see everything in the moment from the perspective of that belief. As a result, you're not open to whatever arises in the moment. You might use reasoning to defend and support your belief. If supporting the belief doesn't work, you might modify your belief, and if that fails, change it entirely. Beliefs must constantly be defended, adjusted, or changed in the face of opposing beliefs, situations, or events. Mounting this defense is painful. It's a resistance against what arises. This conflict with the present situation, this resistance, is suffering.

   • Beliefs must constantly be defended, adjusted, or changed when challenged by doubt generated by opposing beliefs, situations, or events. This defense causes torment because it not only resists the present moment, but it also heightens our sense of separation from others, which is at the very core of our fears and therefore our suffering.

   • Since your beliefs are linked to your identity, you project your beliefs to the outside world. If you believe the world is a terrible place, you will project that vision onto everything you see.

• Because you identify with your beliefs, when what happens doesn't coincide with your belief, you are torn: there's what's happening versus what you believe should be happening.

2. Conflict caused by doubt

• *Belief breeds doubt.* Every belief has an opposing belief. Doubt creates internal conflict, attacking the original belief using the reasoning that supports the opposing belief. Because we identify with our beliefs, we defend them, trying to find better reasoning to conquer our doubt; we modify them in an attempt to outmaneuver our doubt; or we change them altogether.

• Defending your beliefs, not only the deep-rooted beliefs, but even the trivial ones, becomes a matter of defending yourself, because you identify with all your beliefs for as long as you hold them. Therefore there is a constant effort to support your beliefs and prove them to be true, something that is impossible, since thought can never find truth. In effect, maintaining your identity consists of the hopeless task of trying to prove your beliefs beyond a doubt, hoping that somehow you will discover yourself intellectually through the permanence of unwavering truth. This is a process of perpetual self-delusion that leads to depression and other forms of suffering. The beliefs you hold in thought—your very identity—are constantly changing.

• Believing you are your thought is basically believing that you are a lie, and then spending every moment of your life trying to find evidence that will turn that lie into truth. It is a lifetime spent trying to use lies to make other lies true in order to see yourself—your thought-based self—as something other than a lie. This process is hopeless and is experienced as perpetual suffering.

Belief Brings External Conflict

People identify with their beliefs, and for every belief there's an opposite belief. External conflict is created in the clash between people with opposing beliefs.

All external conflict stems from internal conflict.

People are capable of holding on to positive and even negative beliefs for extended periods, even a lifetime, stubbornly fighting their doubts, their experiences, and especially anyone else who opposes their beliefs. This happens because our identities are so deeply wrapped in the belief we are defending that we consider changing our belief, and in some cases even just modifying it slightly, to be a fate worse than death itself. Countless people throughout history have died in defense of their beliefs.

In addition to dealing with doubt internally, using ever stronger reasoning as a countermeasure to the doubt, people also look for allies to support their belief. This is based on the idea that there is strength in numbers—the more people who agree with your belief, the truer it is. Or they attack the people who hold the opposite belief, making them into enemies.

When allies to a belief are found, it is then easier as a group to attack the enemies of the belief.

Many of us feel a strong compulsion to be right. This compulsion arises because we identify with our beliefs. Therefore, defending them as being right is in essence defending ourselves.

In theory, people might say they'd rather be happy than be right, but in practice the opposite is usually the case.

There can be beliefs that have been argued and fought over with the same person or group of people repeatedly, and in some cases for years, or in the case of cultures and countries, even centuries, with no change in perspective and no resolution, and yet the conflict continues. A good example of this is the Israeli–Palestinian conflict. Deep down, neither side is so much interested in changing the opposing belief, it's more a matter of self-defense, which to the individual or group feels like a matter of survival.

The suffering caused by the verbal or physical violence that ensues is obvious to see and examples of external conflicts caused by opposing beliefs are not difficult to find. Just look at the news, here and now or anywhere in the world at any time.

Countries with extreme political beliefs will even resort to torture, not to extract information but to forcibly change their victim's beliefs so that they conform with those of their captors. In the seventeenth century, Japan brutally tortured and murdered hundreds of Japanese Christians including some Jesuit priest missionaries who would not do as they were told and step on images of Jesus Christ or the Virgin Mary. The Japanese believed the spread of Christianity could lead to the kind of colonialism that allowed the Spanish Empire to take control of the Philippines, and therefore wanted to eradicate it.

Belief is used by countries to maintain control over its citizens. In a more recent example, in North Korea, children who have never seen Americans are conditioned to hate them. There is a museum outside of Pyongyang that is devoted to portraying Americans as torturers and warmongers.[5]

When one person commits mass murder, it is easily explained—most people would agree, the killer was insane. But how can anyone account for a group of people committing mass genocide against unarmed victims? What fundamental reason could there be, for example, other than deranged belief, that would incite a vast number of Germany's citizens—in a country that had produced some of the greatest geniuses in philosophy, psychiatry, music, literature, and science—to exterminate 11 million unarmed men, women, and children?

---

5 Jean H. Lee, "How North Korean Children Are Taught to Hate Americans," *Newsweek*, July 6, 2017, http://www.newsweek.com/how-north-korean-children-are-taught-hate-americans-632334.

War is the most extreme example of suffering caused by external conflict. Throughout history, the most horrific wars have been fought in the defense of beliefs.

STORIES OF BELIEF CAUSING SUFFERING

Belief—Internal Conflict—Suffering

PUBLIC SPEAKING

Belief: I am a great speaker.

Situation: I was in college, about to give a speech in front of the entire class. Everyone else had prepared, but for whatever reason, I hadn't thought it at all necessary to do so. I thought it was beneath me, as though the idea of preparing for the speech was akin to riding a bike with training wheels.

When I was a kid, I loved entertaining people. I'd never experienced stage fright and I'd been told repeatedly, and by many people—admittedly relatives—that I was a natural performer and I'd make a great actor. Also, my dad was an awesome speaker. I'd heard him speak at rallies and on TV on many occasions, and somehow, I believed being his son meant I'd inherited his skill set. I didn't really have much else in terms of reasoning to support the belief that I was a great speaker—I'd never once given a formal speech like this one before—but I was still just a teenager, and arrogance trumped a need for justification.

I listened to the other students with pity, their note cards shaking as they held them up to their faces, doing as lousy a job of masking their nervousness as they were at delivering their speeches.

Then it was my turn.

Result: I stood up, back straight, chest out, looked at the crowd before me, paused for dramatic emphasis, and then drew a blank.

I remember the thought I had right then: *No! This isn't possible. This can't be happening to me.*

I stood there, eyes closed, sulking inside, fighting the reality of the moment, hoping if I shut my eyes long enough, when I finally opened them, I'd wake up from this cruel and utterly outrageous nightmare.

When I opened my eyes, instead of seeing my bedroom ceiling, I saw *them*—an entire lecture hall full of students—looking at me with pity. At *me*.

I don't know which was more intense, the feeling of humiliation or that of self-loathing. What made it worse was that I couldn't point the finger of blame at the situation or at anyone else. There was no escaping it—I was responsible for this.

My belief that I was a great speaker was untrue in that moment, and this crushed the self-image I held, leading to lasting internal conflict. It was a blow to my very identity and, as a result, I suffered for days following that event.

Belief—External Conflict—Suffering

THE FIGHT

Belief: The rules of the road were being violated.

Situation: I was walking with my wife in Kolonaki Square, a posh area of Athens, Greece. Just then, a taxi backed up into a guy on a motorbike who was pulling out from the sidewalk, between a barrier and the taxi that was trying to park itself at the back of the line of the taxi stand. The taxi was moving so slowly, it barely even touched the bike and didn't leave a mark.

Result: The motorcyclist got off his bike, inspected his undamaged Honda, and started yelling at the taxi driver for not heeding his warning to stop.

Two other taxi drivers waiting at the taxi stand got out of their taxis and took their colleague's side in the dispute that ensued.

From what I could decipher between swearwords, the motorcyclist was arguing that the driver backing up is responsible to avoid hitting other vehicles or pedestrians, whereas the taxi driver believed the taxi-stand area was off limits for any vehicle other than a taxi, and that anyone operating a non-licensed taxi in this area was violating the law.

In seconds, each party had taken their respective reasoning to extremes: the motorcyclist claimed the taxi driver was intentionally trying to kill him when he was backing up, and the taxi driver insisted that the motorcyclist was destroying their livelihood by scaring off customers.

Each side quickly ran out of reasoning to fuel their respective beliefs. What they lacked in convincing arguments they made up for with expletives and yelling.

Seconds later, the motorcyclist and the taxi driver were exchanging violent blows, hollering insults between breaths.

Another taxi driver joined in to attack the lone motorcyclist in a two-against-one fight, when, out of nowhere, a guy driving a scooter hopped off his bike and took the motorcyclist's side, attacking the two taxi drivers from behind, delivering blows to the back of their heads.

Aside from what the taxi drivers and the motorcyclists were saying, there was no way to discern what each of them believed. Nobody had been injured physically, nor was there damage to property. But the motorcyclist had responded as though his bike had been destroyed and he'd been maimed for life. The taxi driver had been just as outraged.

This was spontaneous, mutual violence caused by a situation that triggered two clearly opposing beliefs.

Out of all the examples of external conflict I could choose from history, the Crusades, World War I, World War II, the Cold War, the Vietnam War, 9/11 and all that ensued thereafter, I chose this mini-conflict precisely because the reasoning underlying the beliefs that caused this violence was absurd enough for there to be no ambiguity that the problem was the belief, not the situation.

Nobody was hurt, no property was damaged—not even slightly. Belief was unquestionably the culprit here. Such violence sparked by such a silly, insignificant event cannot be explained without there being a belief that caused it.

The police were across the street, in their cars, sipping lattes. Had they not been nearby, I got the impression that, given the means, the brawlers might have killed one another.

With fights and arguments, there's always some belief causing the conflict. What that belief is, however, is not as immediately obvious as it may seem. In this case, it appears the men were fighting over the rules of the road. In their arguments, each opposing party claimed the enemy had violated the rules. No injury or damage was caused; it was all imagined: the motorcyclist imagined the *possibility* of getting killed and the taxi driver imagined the *possibility* of losing his customers and therefore his livelihood. I could go deeper with the analysis, but it would only be conjecture. The people involved are the only ones who could uncover their beliefs for themselves. They would have to take a deep look within to find the root cause of their anger.

When we observe fights like this from an emotional distance, they seem nonsensical, and in some cases downright insane. But if we remember times when we were involved in a conflict ourselves— an argument, for example—it is crystal clear to us what we were thinking and believing in each instance, and we can all relate to that compulsion to defend our beliefs by proving them right and attack the opposing belief by proving it wrong.

When we remember our own perspective in a fight, it doesn't seem so insane, at least not at the moment, not while we were believing whatever it was we were believing.

FULFILLMENT ACTION:
SHEDDING BELIEF = SHEDDING SUFFERING

For this fulfillment action, select a powerful negative belief that you have. It can be a personal belief, or one supported by others; it doesn't matter, as long as it generates intense feelings.

Examples of such beliefs might be:

- I'm not worthy.
- I should be doing more with my life.
- I made a terrible mistake when . . .
- We are destroying our planet.
- We're going to be nuked and the survivors will be the unlucky ones.
- The human race won't survive to the next century.

Whatever belief you choose, pick one that really hits home for you. In other words, find something that causes a strong negative emotional reaction when you think the thought.

Repeat the belief to yourself over and over again until you feel the corresponding negative emotion (anger, fear, anxiety, sadness, depression, shame, guilt) has reached a peak.

Now pretend for a moment that the belief is not true. Really feel that. *It isn't true.* Not only is it not true, it's an outright lie.

Nobody wants to believe a lie.

Reject the belief as you would something you just discovered to be a blatant lie.

Let the thought disappear now, as though it is impossible for you to believe it because you know beyond a doubt that it is a lie.

Close your eyes and feel what it's like to no longer believe that thought.

For example: *"I made a terrible mistake."*

Feel that overpowering regret and self-loathing.

Repeat: *"I made a terrible mistake."*

Feel that anger.

Again: *"I made a terrible mistake."*

Experience the tightening in your chest.

Let the feelings hurt until they've reached their peak.

Now see the thought as a lie.

"I made a terrible mistake." NOT TRUE.

Would you believe a lie?

Let the thought be released as you see it for what it is. A lie.

Close your eyes. What does it feel like when you experience the lie for what it is?

4.
What Lies in Truth

SEARCHING FOR TRUTH

My pursuit of enlightenment and my quest for truth were not one and the same until after my experience at Villa di Papà.

I was looking for answers on all subjects, from how to improve myself, especially when it came to handling situations, to finding some unified truth that would explain pretty much everything. The answers I came up with did not stand the test of time. Some would last years, but they all eventually collapsed in face of experience and doubt. Experience invariably showed me that I couldn't devise a formula that worked in every situation. Doubt showed me the many holes in my "unified truth" theories.

There was no way to protect myself—no way to outthink suffering.

When it came to ultimate truth, I didn't want to compromise. However, because I believed in degrees of truth, this was a problem. I did not see thoughts as either true or untrue—there was a gigantic gray area between these two extremes. I failed to come up with a single truth that couldn't be refuted.

Trying to find something to believe that was irrefutably true was a way of searching for the unchanging in the ever-changing. In the sense that change equates to death, my compulsion to find truth was a kind of search for immortality.

My attempts to find truth in thought were futile, since every thought has an opposing thought and therefore could not be ultimately true.

Transcendental Meditation

Through Transcendental Meditation (TM) I had several experiences of what is referred to as pure consciousness. I have no recollection of the experience itself. No memory whatsoever, because there were no thoughts, images, sounds, or sensations to remember. There was no sense of time either. I would look at the clock and fifty minutes may have gone by in what seemed like no time at all. Sometimes more, sometimes less, but there was no difference in the experience. All I recall are the moments just before and just after transcending. The feeling was one of great expansion. Of floating. Awareness of awareness. Pure energy. It is impossible to put the experience into words.

Villa di Papà

In 1998, for a brief while, I experienced everything as true. During this experience, there was no doubt. No paradox. There was just an irrefutable certainty.

After the experience, doubt came in and took it apart completely on an intellectual level. But I couldn't deny the experience of it. It was as undeniable as my experiences of pure consciousness during TM.

Then, in 2016, I experienced everything as untrue. During that experience, there was no doubt or sense of paradox. Instead, there was an intense clarity and certainty similar to my Villa di Papà experience. This time, however, was different in that it came after discovering the ITTIL technique. Being a technique, not a philosophy, ITTIL didn't answer questions of why or how—it didn't offer explanations of any kind, and so there was nothing for my intellect to attack. That everything was untrue was itself untrue. There was no place for doubt, because the ITTIL technique didn't lay any claim to truth.

These three experiences: TM, seeing every thought as true, and then seeing every thought as equally untrue, all have one basic thing in common. Truth was never ascertained by thought. Truth was experienced. Truth was in the experiencing of itself.

What I discovered is that truth is never added—it is always there. Truth comes when what veils it—belief—is removed.

This process is impossible to fully grasp through thoughts, because truth is that which transcends thinking. Truth can only be an experience; it can never be understood.

The good news is that there is a way to experience it for yourself through the ITTIL technique.

TRUTH AND LIES

Conventional truth is what we have learned since the time we started to speak. It is that which is upheld by society, taught in classrooms, and practiced in the workplace, in science, in judicial systems, and pretty much everywhere else.

A conventional lie involves deceiving yourself or others. A lie is an intentional attempt to persuade others to believe something to be true when you do not believe it to be so. In the case of lying to yourself, some psychologists argue it could be intentional or unintentional. Those who maintain that the phenomenon of lying to yourself is unintentional typically also assume the existence of an unconscious.

Conventional Truth
OBJECTIVE TRUTH

1. There are certain objective truths, and these are called facts. These facts have been proven to be true for now; however,

they may prove to be false if the criteria supporting them were to change. (For example, when the definition of what a planet is changed, it altered what previously were considered facts—"Pluto is a planet" and "there are nine planets in our solar system"—into statements that were no longer true.)

2. The methodology for verifying objective truth can be thought based, as long as the underlying presumptions are commonly agreed upon. So the statement "No human can survive on the surface of the sun" need not be proven by sending a person to their doom, but can be established as fact given other facts in physics and biology, and the imagined scenario.

3. Objective truths can be relative and based on certain assumptions.

4. Something can be established as truth by its very definition. Because this is an insidious process, its importance is often overlooked. For instance, one might say that it is a given that we have a mind, an ego, and an unconscious. But there is no evidence to support the validity of these claims.

SUBJECTIVE TRUTH

1. Subjective truth cannot be proven and therefore cannot be disproven.

2. The presumption of subjective truth is often based on the incentive—or lack thereof—to lie. So, in a court of law, if a witness under oath were to say, "I had a migraine," it might be accepted as truth, given the disincentive of the witness in question of perjuring herself over a minor statement. Meanwhile, if someone with young children were to make a similar statement to their employer, offering it as a reason that they did not come to work on Christmas Day, the employer would likely question the veracity of that statement because of the incentive to lie.

3. If we believe something to be true, then, at least to us, it is true. And if we convey this truth to others, their beliefs will dictate whether they perceive it as factually true, partially true, or not true.

4. There are many layers of truth, just as there are many perspectives on what is true.

In a modern-day court, a witness could be asked to swear to tell the truth, the whole truth, and nothing but the truth, and under that oath, might have little hesitation in verifying that the person at the table is indeed the defendant and agree that this is indeed a statement of fact.

When questioned about the woman at the table, were the witness to say, "She is beautiful," it would be considered an opinion, not a statement of fact. But though the statement is an opinion, as long as the witness believes the woman is beautiful, he would still be considered as having told the truth to the extent that he has no perceived incentive to lie.

The conventional definition of truth works for science, the court system, and in many cases in everyday life.

However only the definition of truth given in this book works for the ITTIL technique.

A Conventional Lie

The dictionary definition of a lie is "a false statement made with deliberate intent to deceive; an intentional untruth; a falsehood."

As with conventional truth, conventional lies come in degrees, from white lies used to protect people from harm to downright malicious lies.

The degree to which a lie is considered acceptable is highly subjective.

The dictionary definition may be the conventional use of the word lie (see the section "What Lies in Lies" later in this chapter), but that is not the kind of lie being referred to in the title of this book.

DROPPING CONDITIONING

Conditioning starts the day we learn our very first word. From the moment we are taught to identify objects with labels, we are taught the beginnings of separation. This sense of separation grows as our conditioning grows.

Children are elated when they first experience the power of the spoken word. They can see themselves in relationship to other people and things. A sense of a separate "me" grows even stronger as the ability to differentiate through adjectives is acquired. *Big* woman, *small* boy, *pretty* toy. *Yellow* shirt.

While this fundamental conditioning quickly moves into a more-subjective realm, the majority of children are not taught to distinguish between practical and psychological thoughts.

- Brown dog. *Bad* dog.
- *Pretty* black cat. *Good* cat.

At the same time, children are judged by their actions, and, thirsting for attention and craving praise, they adjust their behavior accordingly.

Good job! Here's a sticker! You won an award!

Soon these constructs, comparisons, and judgments evolve with supporting reasoning. Cindy is a good girl *because* she helped her daddy with the dishes. Bobby is a good boy *because* he picked up his toys.

The deepest conditioning arises during these early childhood years, first with basic practical thoughts, then with elemental, psychological thoughts.

And from there, labels, comparisons, and judgments evolve into stories.

During our childhood, as part of the process of growing, we absorb what we learn from our parents and accept it as truth.

Later on, at home and in school, children are taught to believe and support their own ideas and opinions.

When children grow into teenagers, they search for their identities, seeking out and latching onto beliefs—oftentimes destructive ones—that define them and their self-image. Their self-image is founded on what they believe others believe about them. Each belief that makes up their story squeezes them into a smaller and smaller box. The baggage they carry grows heftier with each passing year.

It's no wonder children seem happier compared to most adults, who, after two decades or more of conditioning, seem miserable.

The ITTIL technique works to dismantle all belief, and therefore conditioning, one thought at a time. Initially, the focus of the practice is on eradicating the conditioning that results in negative psychological thoughts. In advanced applications, the practice deals with conditioning that causes us to believe practical thoughts, from those acquired in recent years through books, through schooling, career, all kinds of education and daily experience, to the deepest conditioning of all—conditioning that was entrenched in us from the day we spoke our very first word.

There are many conventional methods for dropping our conditioning. Most of them target specific conditionings. For instance, some target addictions and compulsions; others target prejudice. Many work to change our negative self-image.

These approaches may help, but their effectiveness is greatly limited, and little is accomplished in the long run to alleviate suffering.

The optimum approach is not to selectively target types of conditioning, but to target belief itself, because belief is behind all conditioning and it is what causes suffering.

This is precisely what the ITTIL technique does. It is the only technique I am aware of that eliminates all belief, thereby freeing us from the conditioning that stems from the most subjective psychological thoughts to the most basic practical thoughts and everything in between.

DEFINING TRUTH

The dictionary offers many definitions of the word "truth."

For the purposes of this book truth is defined in terms of what it is not.

1. Truth has no opposite.
2. There are no degrees of truth.
3. Truth is not relative.

- Truth is not relative to time.
  (It was true in the past. It is true in the present moment. It will be true in the future.)

- Truth is not relative to a perceiver.
  (It's true for me, but not for you.)

- Truth is not relative to space.
  (It's true here, but not there.)

- Truth is not relative to, and doesn't rely on, any assumption.

This definition of truth is essential for the understanding of this book and for the application of the ITTIL technique.

There might be a temptation to disagree with the definition of truth given here. You are welcome to choose any definition you like, but in order for this book to be useful, for the application of ITTIL and for this application only, the definition of truth must be limited to what's given here.

It is not a *true* definition, because it is born of thought. But it is beneficial.

LOOKING AT TRUTH

Properly classifying and defining all the conventional approaches to truth (realism, rationalism, analytic and reductive empiricism, and so on) would fill a small library. What is offered here pertaining to conventional truth is a simplification for comparative purposes. This book is not a philosophical dissertation about truth or any other subject. While conventional truth is contradictory, confusing, and sometimes beneficial and sometimes not, the ITTIL definition is short, simple to understand, and it is always beneficial when it comes to practicing the ITTIL technique.

The conventional approach assumes that truth exists in an objective reality and that we are subjective observers of that reality. It further assumes that there are degrees to understanding truth and, therefore, the way to get "closer" to the truth is through a process of gathering evidence. The quality of the evidence rests in its ability to refute contradiction over a period of time. The quantity of the evidence is the number of instances or observers that confirm something to be true. The better the quality and the higher the quantity, the closer a statement is to the truth.

The ITTIL definition of truth simply, clearly, and definitively states what truth is not.

To illustrate the differences between the conventional and ITTIL approaches to truth, I'll use an example of a Kafkaesque undertaking to get my wife her green card.

Proving Our Marriage Was "Real"
THE CONVENTIONAL APPROACH TO TRUTH

In order to get a permanent residency visa for my wife, the burden was on her (the applicant) to prove the validity of our marital union. The immigration authorities (USCIS) required evidence that the marriage was bona fide or "real," and that we were genuinely in love and intended on staying together forever.

The methodology for establishing this bona fide reality was aligned with the conventional approach and definitions of truth.

Our marriage certificate did not prove anything, because a couple intending on committing fraud could presumably obtain one as easily as we did. It was only useful in applying for the visa, not in obtaining it.

At the time of the application, my wife was five months pregnant. This was considered strong evidence that we intended to stay together for a long time. This is because the usual incentive for any fraudulent marriage is money. The person wanting the green card pays the US citizen to enter in a fraudulent marital union in exchange for a typically large sum. As a captain for a major airline, I was already making a decent income. If this were a fraudulent marriage, how much money would my partner-in-fraud have to pay in order to get me to marry her, have a child with her, and live with her for at least three years? And why would she pay me when she could have easily found some poor guy with a US passport that would have done a lot more for a lot less!

Having a child together made for quality evidence, but it was only *one* child. Now, if we'd had two children, or even better, three, the evidence would have been overwhelming.

As it happened, with just one child, the USCIS was not satisfied. We had to produce photographs from the time we first met, photographs of our wedding showing many guests (the more the merrier, because it is presumed to be difficult to find fake guests for a photo shoot), and photographs of our honeymoon. We were asked to produce evidence in the form of notarized written affidavits from people who knew both of us for more than two years to serve as testimony to our bona fide marital union. And yet still this was not enough. We needed to show commitment in terms of shared assets, including the house, bank accounts, car ownership, life insurance policies, and family health coverage from my employer.

The point of all this evidence was to show that the commitment in time and money far outweighed any reasonable incentive for entering into a fraudulent marriage for the purposes of obtaining a permanent residency visa.

Even though it may sound ludicrous to prove a bona fide "real" marriage with intentions to stay together forever, after looking at the overwhelming quality and quantity of the supporting evidence, from a conventional perspective, it's hard not to draw the conclusion that we were the genuine article after all. Given the standards of evidence for legal purposes, it is possible to prove a lot of things to be true, even things as highly subjective as personal love.

THE ITTIL APPROACH TO TRUTH

Instead of attempting to prove something to be true, the ITTIL technique works by showing what is *not* true.

Its purpose is to dismantle belief in a thought, not to serve as a legal tool, so it wouldn't be used in an attempt to show that the marriage is legitimate, because doing so would create belief, not dismantle it. In order to draw a comparison between the conventional approach to truth and the ITTIL approach, instead of trying to prove the statement "This is a bona fide marital union" true, the ITTIL definition of truth will be used to show that the statement "This is a fraudulent marital union" is *not* true.

"This is a fraudulent marital union" fails all three conditions of the ITTIL definition of truth:

1. Truth has no opposite. "This is a fraudulent marital union" has an opposite that says, "This is *not* a fraudulent marital union," and therefore it is not true.

2. Truth has no degrees. There could conceivably be varying degrees of truth to this statement. For instance, "This is a semi-fraudulent marital union." This could occur if we'd had no romantic love for each other but we were friends with benefits who both happened to want a child, and we both suspected the marriage wouldn't last more than three years. Just enough time to have a little fun playing family and for my wife to get her green card. This is admittedly unlikely, but in order for there to be degrees of truth, the condition doesn't have to be plausible, just possible. Because the statement "This is a fraudulent marital union" can have degrees of truth, it is not true.

3. Truth is not relative. The intention to defraud the US government for the purposes of obtaining a green card is clearly relative. On my part, it would be relative to my desire for money counterbalanced by my reluctance to commit a crime. On the part of my co-conspirator, the intention to defraud would be relative to her desire to acquire permanent residency in the United States in exchange for a small fortune counterbalanced by the possibility of being kicked out of the country forever should things go south at some point in the process. Desires come and go. It is conceivable that initially the plan was to defraud the government, but at some point in time we actually fell in love and ours would become a bona fide marriage (I seem to recall a romantic comedy with that very theme). Therefore, desires are relative both to the perceiver and to time. Because the statement "This is a fraudulent marital union" is relative, it is not true.

To be clear, *this is not an example of the application of the ITTIL technique.* It is an illustration of how conventional truth and the truth for the purposes of ITTIL differ. The conventional approach uses evidence in an attempt to show how the statement "This is a bona fide marriage" is true. The ITTIL approach shows how the statement "This is a fraudulent marital union" is *not* true.

FULFILLMENT ACTION: IDENTIFYING TRUTH

Identifying Conventional Truth

Write down at least three statements that you could make in court, under oath, that you are sure would be accepted as true. (They don't have to be about yourself. They could be laws of physics. Choose any three statements that could be given as evidence and accepted by all parties as factual.)

These statements serve as good examples of conventional truths.

Looking at the ITTIL definition of truth, note how each of the statements you have written fails at least one of the three conditions, making all three conventionally accepted "facts" untrue.

Experiencing the ITTIL Definition of Truth

With ITTIL, truth is experienced, not discovered by thought. Thoughts may arise, but they arise in the background of having the experience. It is the experience that is truth.

When you are in a safe, quiet place, where you know you won't be disturbed for at least thirty seconds, close your eyes and observe your thoughts as though they were bubbles in a fish tank. Don't hold on to any thought; don't follow any thought; don't resist any thought. For these thirty seconds, no thought is more important than another. Consider all thoughts equally meaningless. Feel the empty space in which thoughts arise. At the end of those thirty seconds, ask the question, "What is it that was aware of those thoughts?"

Is there any correlation with this experience just now and a time in your life where you were completely "in the zone," and lost in the moment, a time where you weren't caught up in a single thought, where you became one with your action or inaction?

You will find that truth cannot be identified, it cannot appear as an object known by thought, and therefore it cannot be adequately described with words.

WHAT LIES IN LIES

A lie is that which is not true according to the ITTIL technique definition of truth, but the converse does not apply—**the opposite of a lie is not truth, it's another lie**.

For example, let us look at the following statement: "The universe is expanding."

This statement has an opposite; therefore it is a lie. (Any statement need fail only one of the three criteria of truth in order to be considered false.)

The opposite of the lie "The universe is expanding" is not truth, it is another lie: "The universe is *not* expanding." Of course, this second statement has an opposite as well (the original statement) and so *both* statements are lies.

Statements that have opposites are considered *equally untrue* for the purposes of the ITTIL technique.

Since all statements have opposites, *all statements are equally untrue*.

Seeing if a statement has an opposite is the easiest, fastest way to identify a lie.

However, in order for a statement *not* to be a lie, it would have to satisfy all three criteria of truth:

1. Truth has no opposite.
2. There are no degrees of truth.
3. Truth is not relative to anything.

LOOKING AT LIES

Conventional Lies

A man tells his wife the following: "I was in my hotel room at 9:00 last night."

Let's say that he remembers actually being at the bar at that time.

This would be considered a conventional lie because the man is intentionally trying to get his wife to believe something he knows is not true.

Let's change the situation slightly and say that the same man remembers being at the bar at 7:00 p.m. but believes that he left the bar for his hotel room two hours later, when in fact he had remained at the bar until 9:45. In this case, while what the man is saying is still untrue, it is not considered a conventional lie because the man misremembers the facts and there is no intention to deceive.

Lies According to the ITTIL Definition of Truth

Let us say this time the man tells his wife, "I was at the bar at 9:00 last night," and there were half a dozen people who could verify that statement. Due to the supporting evidence, convention would consider this a true statement, however it would still fail the ITTIL definition of truth:

1. Because whereas truth has no opposite, the statement above does. The opposite is: "I was *not* at the bar at 9:00 last night."

2. Truth is not relative. The statement is relative to the observer, the observer's location (the bar), and finally it is relative to time (*at 9:00* last night).

———

All conventional lies are also lies according to the ITTIL definition. However, not all lies according to the ITTIL definition are necessarily lies according to the conventional definition.

Put simply, a conventional lie is any thought or statement that intentionally deceives, whereas for the purposes of ITTIL, no thought or statement can be true and therefore all thoughts are lies.

FULFILLMENT ACTION: IDENTIFYING LIES

Write three statements that would be considered by almost anyone to be a lie.

For example: *All babies are born with golden wings.*

Write three statements that would be considered by almost everyone to be true.

For example: *The sun is a star.*

Using the ITTIL definition of truth, *without using conventional reasoning*, show how all six statements are untrue.

5.
The ITTIL Technique

THEN AND NOW

Checkrides

BEFORE ITTIL

As I have mentioned earlier, I am an airline captain. Pilots undergo periodic proficiency evaluations referred to in aviation jargon as checkrides. For the most part, for professional pilots, checkrides involve annual or semiannual periodic checks. Depending on the checkride, the consequences of not passing can vary. In most cases, second and even third attempts are possible, however the stress and anxiety of retaking a checkride is typically much higher with each retake. Also, failing or "busting" a checkride remains on a pilot's record permanently.

I used to always have anxiety before a checkride. The only remedy I had for my nervousness was to study. So I hit the books to the point where I felt I knew as much about the jet and procedures as I could possibly retain. That level of preparation entailed four to six weeks of studying eight hours a day, seven days a week.

While I was studying, I would put everything else, including family, on hold. My thinking was that if I were to do anything other than study—such as go to the gym, read a book (forget writing one), or go to a movie with my kids—I'd risk missing something in my studies, thereby jeopardizing my family's financial future. After all, this reasoning went, how could I possibly support a family of five in any other profession?

For my Boeing 737 type rating, I studied for two months, and in 2007, when I upgraded to captain, I studied for three.

Then when I returned to flying after four years of being on medical disability, I planned to study for two months, but because of the government shutdown in the fall of 2013, there was a long delay before the FAA gave me my medical certificate, and so I ended up studying for almost four months straight, every single day, no exceptions, just to keep all the information I'd accrued fresh in my memory. That was the most draining study marathon I'd ever experienced.

All that preparation greatly reduced my anxiety, but I still dreaded the checkrides that would follow the five weeks of retraining that was required for me to resume flying as a captain again.

I overstudied prior to checkrides because my performance typically dropped to 80 percent due to nerves, and that was on a good day.

Most of the time, one or two nights before a checkride, I'd have difficulties sleeping. The night before I'd be lucky to get six hours of sleep. I'd be so stressed and tired following a checkride, I'd often get a nasty cold the very next day.

AFTER ITTIL

Normally, I have my annual proficiency checks in late November, but in 2017, the training scheduling department set me up for a checkride in the first days of that month, a full two weeks earlier than usual.

Due to this unforeseen change, instead of having my usual five weeks to study, that year, I had but two. In the past, I would have been suffering serious stress. I'd have shut down everything else in my life and started cramming at the library until the day of my checkride, studying through sleepless nights in the process.

That year, I studied less than I had before any checkride I can recall since I started flying, almost thirty years earlier.

I hit the books for about two hours a day, and not every day. I found time to attend a Science & Non-Duality conference, read a few books, continue writing the first edition of this book, be with my family, and practice the piano.

In Dallas, where our checkrides are held, I actually met up with a family friend the night before. We didn't stay up late, of course, but we did have fun. I slept like a baby, and the next day I had the easiest, most relaxed checkride of my life. I saw it as a great learning experience, which is precisely the training center's goal for these evaluations.

All the nervousness, apprehension, anxiety, and sleepless nights that I'd experienced in the past were due to some thought I was believing about what might happen were I to fail the checkride. These thoughts no longer seem to arise for me, but were they to do so, I'd simply apply the ITTIL technique, drop my belief in those thoughts, and free myself of the associated suffering.

A Matter of a Course

BEFORE ITTIL

For most of my life, I believed that science was the best, most logical, methodology for uncovering truth.

It made no sense to me that brilliant people, especially brilliant scientists, could also be religious. Jesus walking on water and performing all these other miracles? How could smart people believe such things?

On a cold November day in Dallas, many years ago, a friend for whom I had the deepest respect told me she was reading a book called *A Course in Miracles*.

I wasn't really looking for any new path, as I was in the early stages of formulating the ITTIL technique. Nevertheless, out of curiosity, I purchased the book and started reading.

I didn't get through the first page.

The prose seemed bombastic, arrogant, and presumptuous. The author—presumably channeling from a voice that identified himself as Jesus—states the following in the very first paragraph: "This is a course in miracles. It is a required course. Only the time you take it is voluntary."

What imperiousness!

I felt as though I were reading religious dogma blended in with New Age nonduality but fashioned in a paradoxically dualistic manner to accommodate religious terms found in the Bible. It made no sense to me whatsoever. The language was unnecessarily archaic and overwrought, to the point of outdoing legal texts in its use of the passive voice.

I put the book aside, dismissing it as annoying gibberish, and I wondered how my friend could possibly endure such pompous dogma.

AFTER ITTIL

As my practice of ITTIL deepened within me, my resistance to religion started to relax. One could believe in Euclidian geometry or in the stories of Jesus curing lepers. A belief was a belief. No belief was really more or less ludicrous than any other; it was only believed to be so.

This, I saw, had nothing to do with faith—because faith transcended explanation, whereas belief always relied on reason. And ultimately, reason cannot support Euclidian geometry any more than it can support the miracles in the New Testament.

From this new perspective, I wondered why many priests found it necessary to use reasoning to get their parishioners to believe. It seemed to me that only the unfaithful need to believe.

Once there is faith, belief becomes petty and meaningless.

It no longer seemed odd that brilliant scientists could also be Christians, Buddhists, Hindus, or Muslims. If they had faith, they would have no need for belief and the nonsensical reasoning that supported it.

Around that time, I decided to take another look at *A Course in Miracles* (*ACIM*).

Many of my Facebook followers were dedicated to *ACIM*, and because my friend was so involved, out of curiosity, I started reading once again.

According to *ACIM*, belief is not a requirement, and that was all I needed to proceed. I was surprised that I was no longer bothered by what I was reading. Actually, I saw great beauty in the words.

I was not reading out of any need to attain anything, for there was nothing that it could offer me that wasn't readily available right then, in the moment. As I read, I simply enjoyed.

I read *ACIM* for the sake of reading *ACIM*. If I noticed even the slightest resistance, I looked for a lingering belief that was popping up from my past that was resisting what I was reading. Only a belief can cause resistance. After finding the resistance, the ITTIL technique released me from this fleeting bond with the belief, and I was freed from it. What I experienced in the reading was an opening to the moment, a wonderful blessing.

Prior to ITTIL, I would have been shocked—and probably a little frightened—were Future Me to come back and say that I was reading *ACIM*. I would have been scared because I would have thought Future Me was actually believing it. Like most people, Past Me believed that the problem was caused by what I was believing, not in the act of believing itself.

This isn't to say that because of ITTIL I would necessarily read or partake in everything that I'd have normally resisted in the past. I am open now, but of the many options available, there are those that are beneficial to me in the moment and others that are not.

Being open doesn't mean you lose your personal preferences! For example, if you preferred French vanilla to pistachio ice cream prior to ITTIL, after practicing the technique, you won't necessarily find yourself suddenly liking pistachio ice cream as well!

THE ITTIL TECHNIQUE

How the Pieces Fit Together

We have looked at thoughts, beliefs, and truth from both a conventional perspective and from the ITTIL perspective.

A conventional model of thinking would follow in this manner:

> *Thought → Unquestioned acceptance of the thought → Belief → Perceived Truth → Doubt → Conflict (internal and external) → Suffering*

The thought process with the ITTIL technique looks as follows:

> *Apply the ITTIL technique on the thought you are believing → See the thought and its opposite as equally untrue → Determine if the thought is beneficial*

The ITTIL technique is based on the idea that **all thoughts are equally untrue.**

It is important to understand that this statement itself is *not* a belief. It is, in itself, not true. It is the foundation of the ITTIL technique, however, and as such it is beneficial—essential, really—because without it, the technique simply doesn't work.

When to Apply the ITTIL Technique

Short Answer: *Whenever you find yourself believing a thought.*

How do you know you believe a thought?

- When you sense even the slightest resistance to the present moment.
- When you have a sense of desire, lack, or longing.
- When you find yourself seeking truth, or even just an explanation.

- When you're using thought to find some philosophical
  or spiritual truth, scientific truth, or truth of any kind.
- When you feel the need to defend or support a thought.

1. Use ITTIL on psychological thoughts
- When you have a recurring thought that you can't seem
  to shake.
- When you have a thought that doesn't feel beneficial.
- When you are feeling anger, fear, anxiety, sadness,
  depression, shame, or guilt, and you associate this with
  a negative thought.

Basically, use ITTIL when you experience a negative psychological reaction to any thought you are believing.

(In the early stages of the practice, the ITTIL technique is applied only to negative psychological thoughts. In advanced applications, the ITTIL technique can be used on *all* psychological thoughts, including thoughts that are considered positive, or thoughts that appear to be practical in nature.)

2. Use ITTIL to end seeking
- When you're thinking of using a technique, method,
  or path you believe will make you better than what you
  are right now.
- When you're using thought to find some philosophical
  or spiritual explanation, truth, scientific truth, or truth
  of any kind.
- When you find yourself believing thoughts, and by extension
  paths or techniques, that seek fulfillment, happiness, truth,
  or anything considered lacking, *especially* enlightenment,
  sometime in the imaginary future.

(More on this in the next chapter.)

3. Use ITTIL to end all belief

Your last beliefs are shed in this application, and so using ITTIL for this purpose comes in the final stages of the practice. These are the beliefs upon which most people base their identity—the idea of their own separate existence.

To give you an idea of what these beliefs might be, here's a short list:

- The belief in the story of you—a you with a beginning (birth) and an end (death).
- The belief in a you made up of a series of past events and future aspirations and hopes.
- The belief in a you who only exists in imagination.
- The belief in a separate you who can observe an external "reality."
- The belief in a future enlightened you.
- The belief in an unenlightened you.
- The belief in the necessity of belief itself.

(More on this in the next chapter.)

THE ITTIL TECHNIQUE

1. Identify the thought opposite to the one you are believing.

2. Use the opposite thought along with reasoning to negate the original thought, and stop when both thoughts are seen as *equally untrue.* (In order for this to be effective, it is essential to use *convincing* reasoning that *resonates for you.*)

3. Determine if and how either thought could be beneficial to you at this moment.

ITTIL TECHNIQUE EXAMPLES

Now that we have had a first look at the ITTIL technique, I will apply it on a few of the previous stories to demonstrate how it works on a practical level.

I AM SPECIAL

Summary: I believed that I was special and that people loved me for that reason.

APPLYING THE ITTIL TECHNIQUE

I can identify two thoughts here (1) "I am special," and (2) "People love me because I'm special."

First thought: "I am special."

STEP ONE: Find the thought opposite to the one you are believing.

- "I am *not* special."

STEP TWO: Use the opposite thought along with reasoning to negate the original thought, and stop when both thoughts are seen as *equally untrue*. (In order for this to be effective, it is essential to use *convincing* reasoning that *resonates for you*.)

Supporting reasoning: Everyone considers themselves to be special, or at least different. In that regard, I'm no different.

There are degrees of specialness. I might be somewhat special if I spoke two languages, more special if I spoke five, and presumably most special if I spoke them all. Truth has no degrees, therefore being special is not true.

Everything that I believed made me special is fleeting.

It is dependent on time.

It is dependent on the observer.

Truth is not relative, therefore my being special is *not* true.

"I am special" has an opposite, "I am *not* special."

Truth has no opposite, therefore neither statement is true.

STEP THREE: Determine if and how either thought could be beneficial to you at this moment.

- "I am special." Not true.
- "I am *not* special. Not true.

Of the two untrue statements, I find "I am *not* special" would have been most beneficial at the moment because it would free me from the belief in separateness.

Second thought: "People love me because I am special."

STEP ONE: Find the thought opposite to the one you are believing.

- "People do *not* love me because I'm special."

STEP TWO: Use the opposite thought along with reasoning to negate the original thought, and stop when both thoughts are seen as *equally untrue*. (In order for this to be effective, it is essential to use *convincing* reasoning that *resonates for you*.)

Supporting reasoning: The statement assumes that I know why people love me. However, most people who tell me they love me don't give me any reasons.

It further assumes that there need be a reason to love. It also presumes some definition of love.

Other people, me, my presumed specialness—all these things are time-dependent. Therefore they are relative.

Truth is not relative, and so the statement is not true.

STEP THREE: Determine if and how either thought could be beneficial to you at this moment.

- "People love me because I am special." Not true.
- "People do *not* love me because I'm special." Not true.

Of the two untrue statements, I find "People do *not* love me because I'm special" would have been most beneficial at that moment, because by using that thought there would have been no compulsion to do anything for the purpose of being loved.

CERTAIN DEATH

Summary: I was alone after surgery, and testing had just shown I had a clot that I believed would soon kill me.

APPLYING THE ITTIL TECHNIQUE

Finding the thought behind my fear is easy: "I'm going to die soon."

Finding the thought behind my anger is also easy: "I have the right to know when I'm going to die."

Thought behind my fear: "I'm going to die soon."

STEP ONE: Find the thought opposite to the one you are believing.

- "I'm *not* going to die soon."

STEP TWO: Use the opposite thought along with reasoning to negate the original thought, and stop when both thoughts are seen as *equally untrue.* (In order for this to be effective, it is essential to use *convincing* reasoning that *resonates for you.*)

Supporting reasoning: I'm not going to die soon, because if I were, presumably they wouldn't be leaving me here in the corridor alone for my last hour alive. Hospitals, doctors, and medical professionals are paranoid about lawsuits. They get patients to sign forms for everything. Leaving a doomed patient alone after the doctors had determined my condition, with proof they knew about the blood clot, would have given my mother ample ammunition and a very good chance of scoring some serious money in a lawsuit. It would be a slam-dunk case. No way would they knowingly allow this.

I had no evidence to support the belief I would die soon. All I knew was my surgeon had recently had a similar case and the patient was now dead. The surgeon wasn't clear as to how long it had taken his patient to die, nor had he stated how long it might take me to die were I to get a clot.

At this point I found sufficient reasoning to neutralize my belief in the original thought and see that both the original and opposite thoughts were equally untrue.

STEP THREE: Determine if and how either thought could be beneficial to you at this moment.
- "I am going to die soon." Not true.
- "I am *not* going to die soon." Not true.

The second thought, "I am *not* going to die soon," would clearly have been more beneficial to me in that corridor. I was immobilized on a mobile hospital bed with no ability to do anything constructive. I couldn't even take notes if an interesting thought were to arise. It was shortly after surgery and I was still medicated through an IV. I wasn't thinking straight, so even if I had the means to take notes, it was highly unlikely I'd come up with anything worth writing down.

Believing the thought that I was going to die soon, I was plagued with anger and fear and this caused panic and more negative thoughts to arise. Using the thought that I was not going to die soon (without believing it), I would have an opportunity to clear my thoughts and allow myself some much-needed rest.

Thought behind my anger: "I have the right to know when I'm going to die."

STEP ONE: Find the thought opposite to the one you are believing.
- "I do *not* have the right to know when I'm going to die."

STEP TWO: Use the opposite thought along with reasoning to negate the original thought, and stop when both thoughts are seen as *equally untrue*. (In order for this to be effective, it is essential to use *convincing* reasoning that *resonates for you*.)

Supporting reasoning: The assumption is that the doctors knew when I was going to die and were not telling me. My surgeon hadn't specified how long it would take for me to die, so he might not have even known. In which case, if he didn't know, then how would anyone else? And if no one else knew, then how could I believe I had a right to know something that simply wasn't known?

Also, the only doctors that I could be certain knew about my clot were the ones consulting behind the glass. I did not know their specialties. It is likely that none of them were surgeons. If that were the case, then what made me think any of them would know that a clot such as this one immediately following a splenectomy meant death at any point in time?

Even if they did know, they may have assumed that the guy transporting me had already taken me back to my room. They may have had no knowledge that I was stuck there in the corridor for so long. They may have assumed I'd be speaking with my surgeon just minutes after I was released from their care.

At this point I find there's sufficient reasoning to neutralize my belief in the original thought and see that both the original and opposite thoughts are equally untrue.

STEP THREE: Determine if and how either thought could be beneficial to you at this moment.

- "I have the right to know when I'm going to die." Not true.
- "I do *not* have the right to know when I'm going to die." Not true.

Pretty much the same reasoning applies for this thought. Even if I did have the right to know when I was going to die and even if they were able to tell me, I clearly was in no position to demand an answer from anyone. I'd tried, and nobody was there to answer me. I was alone and I didn't know how much longer I'd remain alone. It could have been hours, it could have been a matter of a minute. I was unable to get off the bed and go anywhere. I wasn't able to even think straight.

Believing the thought that I had the right to know when I was going to die was only causing me anger and severe agitation, which obviously wasn't helpful to me on a psychological level and probably was detrimental on a physical level as well.

What I needed was rest, and using the thought that I do not have the right to know when I was going to die (without believing it), I could let go of that line of thinking, relax, and maybe get some repose. Even if I were going to die in the next few minutes, I would have preferred doing so in peace rather than in a state of panic and anger.

THE "I AM THINKING . . ." TECHNIQUE

When to Apply the "I AM THINKING . . ." Technique

Some thoughts that you believe can slip by, unexamined. Like a puppeteer, a thought can remain hidden from view, pulling at your emotional strings, causing anger, fear, anxiety, sadness, depression, shame, or guilt, to name just a few negative feelings.

If you are experiencing psychological suffering with no discernible source, then there are some unnoticed thoughts lurking in the background of your thinking—likely camouflaged among many other thoughts—that are the cause of your suffering.

This is where the "I AM THINKING . . ." technique comes in—it weeds out unexamined thoughts so that you can then use the ITTIL technique to eliminate their negative effects.

THE "I AM THINKING . . ." TECHNIQUE

1. Examine your thoughts, prefacing them with the words "I AM THINKING. . . ." This gives you the space required to step back from your thinking.

2. Observe each underlying thought that led you to the current belief and preface it with "I AM THINKING . . ." until you have probed deeply enough to uncover the precise thought at the core of your current perception.

3. Use the ITTIL technique on that core thought.

The "I AM THINKING . . ." technique is observing your thinking and going deeper until the core thought behind the negative feeling is uncovered. The ITTIL technique is applied, and belief in the thought drops away. If the thought is not beneficial, because it is not true according to the ITTIL definition of truth, there will be no compulsion to cling to it, so it will no longer have a hold over you.

"I AM THINKING . . ." EXAMPLES

The "I AM THINKING . . ." technique is used to root out unexamined thoughts.

It's used whenever you are not feeling at peace or whenever you are feeling some kind of unpleasantness, no matter how slight, and you cannot pinpoint the underlying thought you are believing that is triggering the negative feeling.

Say to yourself, **"I AM THINKING..."**

Always use the present tense. Even though the subject of your thoughts may be something in the past or the future, the thinking itself is occurring now.

Whatever thought arises, say it to yourself.

Example 1

RESTLESS

I'm taking a mandatory recurrent training class at the training center in Dallas. (Pilots are required to attend such classes prior to their checkrides, which take place the following day.)

This class lasts all day. In fact, the instructor giving the class is affectionately referred to as All-Day Ray.

Finding the unpleasant response is easy.

My left foot is pumping up and down like the piston of a Ferrari in fifth gear.

I note this and force myself to stop.

I listen to more information I've heard time and time again. Not only have I heard all this before, I've just spent a solid month studying in preparation for my oral exam tomorrow.

The torture continues.

My right leg starts pumping this time.

While I didn't have the ITTIL technique back then, I can easily apply the technique now to the memory I'm conjuring at this moment.

The ITTIL technique calls for using reasoning to support the opposite thought, but I have to find the thought first in order to find its opposite.

This is where the "I AM THINKING . . ." technique comes in. Homing in on the exact thought that is triggering the unpleasant emotion or reaction is something that improves with practice.

The key is to keep probing until you have exactly the right wording. You'll feel it reverberate inside you. You'll feel that unmistakable "Aha! Exactly!" reaction. It's akin to finding the exact spot to scratch.

When the thought you've found triggers the precise feeling you were experiencing at that moment, then you know you've found the core belief.

In this instance, the feeling was restlessness—a kind of watered-down frustration. An urge to get up and run. Or scream.

That's the feeling, and my body responds by pumping a foot.

So starting off easily and simply, I experience the feeling and see what thought arises and I repeat this process until I've got the exact thought nailed down.

Here it goes:

"I AM THINKING . . . This class is boring."

I let that settle.

Not quite.

I try again.

"I AM THINKING . . . I should be doing something else."

"I AM THINKING . . . I could be doing something else."

Getting much warmer here.

"I AM THINKING . . . I am wasting my time."

"I AM THINKING . . . I don't deserve to be wasting my time."

"I AM THINKING . . . I am better than this."

Bingo!

The distinctions between some thoughts might be subtle. And sometimes, the thought that resonates might be very different from what you expected.

Allow the thought. Don't judge it as stupid, wrong, good, or bad.

The "I AM THINKING . . ." technique is used to locate the precise thought that has triggered the emotion. Nothing more, nothing less.

Don't play psychologist, make the process complicated, or change it in any way.

It's simple: find the thought, then apply the ITTIL technique on that thought.

STEP ONE: Find the thought opposite to the one you are believing.

With the thought identified, "I am better than this," finding the opposite is easy.

- "I am *not* better than this."

STEP TWO: Use the opposite thought along with reasoning to negate the original thought, and stop when both thoughts are seen as *equally untrue.* (In order for this to be effective, it is essential to use *convincing* reasoning that *resonates for you.*)

Supporting reasoning: "I am not better than this" because "better" is completely subjective. "This" is what's happening.

What's happening is the situation: I am pumping my foot.

I cannot be better or worse at the moment. Looking at it closely, the feeling of impatience, frustration, and the foot pumping are not caused by the situation (in this case, the recurrent class I'm attending), it's caused by what I believe about the situation. And I'm believing that I am better than this. Even if there were such a thing as being better than a situation, I clearly am not, since I'm there, pumping my foot!

At this point, looking at that memory, I need no more reasoning for the opposite thought in order to drop the belief in the original thought.

STEP THREE: Determine if and how either thought could be beneficial to you at this moment.

I have the following:

- "I am better than this." Not true.
- "I am *not* better than this." Not true.

I listen in stillness to both untrue thoughts and I find that *neither* is of benefit to me and being equally untrue, I drop them both effortlessly.

Example 2

IRRITABLE

I'm with my wife on a beautiful sunny day prior to learning the ITTIL technique. I've got a few days off from flying and as we drive to our favorite Thai restaurant for lunch, I am thinking about how nice I was being to her for agreeing to have lunch instead of seeing that movie I'd been looking forward to for more than a week.

Looking away from me, she says, "So why are you in such a bad mood? Is it because we're not seeing that movie?"

Me: "*I'm* in a bad mood?" I say, startled by the abrupt tone of my own voice. "*You* must be in a bad mood, because I'm in a great mood, or at least I was until now."

Her: "I kept asking you if you still wanted to go to the Thai place and you wouldn't answer."

Me: "I said yes twice. You weren't listening, as usual. Why do you ask me a question and then walk off and pretend I didn't answer you?"

Her: "Well, I could tell you were in a bad mood because you wanted to see that movie."

Me: "First of all, I never said I was in a bad mood and I never once mentioned the movie."

Her: "Yes, but I can *tell*."

Me: "I promise you, I was in a great mood. In fact, I was just thinking about what a great mood I was in, but you spoiled everything with your passive-aggressive button-pushing."

Her: "I hate it when you say 'button-pushing.'"

Me: "*Button-pushing, button-pushing, button-pushing.* It's what you do. You're the button-pushing master. Nobody pushes my buttons better than you."

I don't remember the exact words. I do seem to recall we managed to survive lunch.

Taking myself back to that scene, the feelings I was having are clear to me, but what isn't immediately evident is the thought that I was believing that had triggered the feelings of outrage and injustice.

At this point, I would apply the "I AM THINKING . . ." technique.

"**I AM THINKING** . . . she ruined my good mood."

"**I AM THINKING** . . . I was in a great mood and she pushed my buttons for no reason and with no provocation."

"**I AM THINKING** . . . she said I was in a bad mood because of the movie, but not only did I not mention the movie, I was willing to go along with her change of plans and have lunch instead."

I sit a little with the last thought, because I'm starting to feel a flare-up of irritability.

"**I AM THINKING** . . . she said she wanted to see a movie, then she changed her mind, I was cool with it, and she blamed me on top of everything else."

Warmer.

"**I AM THINKING** . . . she should consider what I want and be grateful to me when I consider what she wants."

That's it!

When I go back and imagine that situation and I factor in this thought I was believing, I get exactly what I was feeling.

I believed I was in a great mood, but in fact I was irritable because of this unexamined thought.

My wife picked up on my body language, triggering the emotional response in me.

Finding the exact thought might be hard at first. And you might be surprised at the emotions that pour out. Don't judge those either. With experience, you'll learn to probe your thoughts more deeply and effectively.

If the thought you come up with doesn't seem quite right, keep adjusting until you find what's really behind your feelings.

Having found the thought, without criticizing or judging myself, I apply the ITTIL technique.

STEP ONE: Find the thought opposite to the one you are believing.

- "She *shouldn't* consider what I want and be grateful to me when I consider what she wants."

STEP TWO: Use the opposite thought along with reasoning to negate the original thought, and stop when both thoughts are seen as *equally untrue*. (In order for this to be effective, it is essential to use *convincing* reasoning that *resonates for you*.)

Supporting reasoning: She can't consider what I want when I don't make it clear what I want. She knew I wanted to see the movie, but I hadn't made it understood how *much* I wanted to do that. I'd accepted the idea of going to the Thai place so casually, she could have assumed I didn't really mind.

I actually *told* her I didn't mind!

How can she be grateful to me when she doesn't even know that I sacrificed my wants out of consideration for hers?

STEP THREE: Determine if and how either thought could be beneficial to you at this moment.

So now I have:

- "She should consider what I want and be grateful to me when I consider what she wants." Not true.

- "She *shouldn't* consider what I want and be grateful to me when I consider what she wants." Not true.

Both statements are equally untrue, and the statement that's beneficial to me at the moment is: "She *shouldn't* consider what I want and be grateful to me when I consider what she wants." If she were to consider what I want and be grateful to me, I wouldn't learn to rely on myself for what I want, and not on others or external situations.

Example 3

BLUES

I walk out of the supermarket, I'm on vacation, and it's another beautiful day.

And yet I'm feeling the blues.

This was a time prior to my discovering the ITTIL technique.

Taking myself back to that situation, I find the thought that's triggering this slight depression is not immediately obvious.

I imagine everything as I remember it. I allow the unpleasantness to rise in me now as it did then.

I am still, allowing whatever thought arises to be seen.

I begin:

"I AM THINKING . . . I'm ungrateful. Everything is wonderful, yet I'm feeling like I want to crawl back into bed."

"I AM THINKING . . . It's a great day, I'm on vacation, what's my problem?"

"I AM THINKING . . . What did I just do?"

"I AM THINKING . . . I just went shopping."

"I AM THINKING . . . I was out of cash and I used my debit card."

"I AM THINKING . . . I'm not following my own budget."

At this point, I've narrowed it down to the budget, but the thought isn't spot-on.

I can feel it's not really the source. So, I adjust the wording until it feels exactly like the cause.

"I AM THINKING . . . I rarely ever make it to the end of the month as planned."

"I AM THINKING . . . the budget is a joke since I'm not following it."

Still not right.

"I AM THINKING . . . I'll never get my finances under control."

There we go!

Don't force these thoughts, with practice you'll find the exact phrasing that is ringing that chord deep within you, triggering the negative emotion.

In this case it happens to be:

- "I'll never get my finances under control."

Now that I've narrowed down the thought, I can apply the ITTIL technique.

STEP ONE: Find the thought opposite to the one you are believing.
- "I'll *not* never get my finances under control."

This is a good example of a double negative. It is clumsy, and normally the original statement would be modified so the opposing statement doesn't sound this way, but I offered this one intentionally to show that, clumsy or not, it still works. This way, by remaining a negation, albeit a double negation, there is no suggestion of truth in the opposite statement.

STEP TWO: Use the opposite thought along with reasoning to negate the original thought, and stop when both thoughts are seen as *equally untrue.* (In order for this to be effective, it is essential to use *convincing* reasoning that *resonates for you.*)

Supporting reasoning: The original thought makes a future prediction, as does the opposite thought.

However, I don't know what will happen in the future.

And since the original thought has an opposite thought, neither thought can be true, as truth has no opposite.

If one thought seems truer than another, then more reasoning needs to be applied to the opposite thought in order to negate both and see them as equally untrue.

STEP THREE: Determine if and how either thought could be beneficial to you at this moment.

- "I'll never get my finances under control." Not true.
- "I'll *not* never get my finances under control." Not true.

Which thought is beneficial?

I'd most likely choose "I'll *not* never get my finances under control." At which point, I could even choose to modify the statement to an empowering question such as, "What will it take to get my finances under control?" or better still, "What will it take to be consistently under budget as of next month?"

To summarize the "I AM THINKING . . ." technique: Simply notice if you are experiencing some form of suffering (anger, depression, reactivity, sadness), or even the most subtle unpleasantness. If there is any form of psychological suffering, there's always an unexamined thought that you're believing that's the culprit.

If you do this consistently, when you feel you are not at peace in the moment, uprooting unexamined thoughts will come so naturally, you may find yourself jumping straight to the ITTIL technique the moment you sense psychological discomfort, having almost immediately identified the underlying thought behind the negative feeling.

REASONS FOR USING REASONING

The ITTIL technique involves using reasoning to support the opposite thought, and this reasoning may or may not include employing the ITTIL definition of truth.

Using the ITTIL definition of truth to eliminate a belief—what is referred to here as *elimination by definition*—is the easiest and fastest method of eliminating belief in a thought. It addresses the thought directly, without supporting the opposite thought, so there is no risk of switching your belief from the original thought to its opposite.

As easy and fast as it is, elimination by definition, when used on its own, is not the most effective method for eradicating belief when it comes to psychological thoughts.

Actually, there are not many thoughts for which this method alone is found to be most effective in the beginning of the practice. Usually, in order for it to work, the hold of the belief must be fairly weak. When the hold of *all* belief is weakened in the much later advanced applications of the ITTIL technique, then elimination by definition starts to be the dominant strategy.

The ITTIL technique uses reasoning to support the opposite thought in order to eliminate belief in the original thought. This is because reasoning is the means by which belief is both engrained and sustained and is therefore the most powerful tool for eliminating belief.

However, if you're not careful, it can be a double-edged sword. What makes reasoning such an effective tool is that it is how belief is created and sustained in the first place. And because reasoning creates belief, using it to remove a belief by supporting an opposite belief means you run the risk of effectively trading one belief for another.

It is therefore essential to gauge the point at which reasoning has been used just enough on the original thought that both the original and the opposite thoughts are seen as *equally* untrue.

Overdoing the reasoning could create an imbalance wherein it would then be necessary to tip the scales in the reverse direction and support the original thought!

The Truth-In-Reasoning Trap

Because we have spent most of our lives worshipping the logic of reasoning and using it to support facts and truth, there is a strong tendency to value that reasoning in the practice of the ITTIL technique beyond its intended purpose.

When helping people with step two of the ITTIL technique, I often get the objection, "Yeah, but what you're saying doesn't prove my belief is wrong."

The point is *not* to prove anything. Doing so isn't even possible! Reasoning is not used to prove, but to dislodge belief.

If you find yourself caught in that trap, remember, the ITTIL technique is not a philosophy. Use elimination by definition to show that your belief doesn't meet the definition of truth for the purposes of the technique. Step out of the story that claims an undeniable truth in what you are believing by reminding yourself that this is a practice, nothing more or less. Trying to find truth on an intellectual level using the ITTIL technique acts as a way of generating belief and therefore suffering, not freeing yourself from it.

Don't trick yourself into thinking the reasoning you use should be correct by some objective standard, or even agreed upon by others. The reasoning is *personal*. If it resonates for you, then that's all the reasoning you need to dislodge the belief. There is no correct reasoning, because reasoning cannot be true; all it can be is beneficial to you in dislodging your belief.

Don't get attached to the opposing reasoning you are using. Let it resonate for you only with respect to the belief you are attempting to dislodge and that is all. Once that is done, let it go. It is just as false as the belief it is eradicating, because reasoning is based on thoughts and all thoughts are equally untrue. So, for example, if science plays a major part in your conditioning, you can counter what you used to believe as facts by using science itself. For instance, you might counter Newtonian physics with relativity or quantum mechanics. The purpose would be to dislodge your belief in Newtonian physics, not solidify your belief in quantum mechanics. If both are seen as untrue, then you are free to use both or neither or just one whenever it is useful to do so.

This is not a debate—its purpose is not to change your opinion or belief. It is to *eliminate* your belief. Because we have been conditioned to think in terms of convincing ourselves or others, in terms of changing others' opinions and beliefs, there tends to be a lot of resistance to using reasoning in this manner.

Vigilance is required to maintain a distance from your reasoning and to use it solely as a tool for dislodging belief.

At some point in the advanced application of the ITTIL technique, elimination by definition will become the predominant method, and eventually the whole process of using reasoning to neutralize belief will become unnecessary.

Just like it isn't necessary to go through all the steps needed to ride a bicycle in order to ride it—and you will manage this with muscle memory or background thoughts—all three steps of the ITTIL technique will come as a package deal, and you won't have to do a thing to see a thought is untrue; it will come automatically.

THE QUESTION OF QUESTIONS

If you are trying to apply ITTIL to a thought that is a question, the first step is to break down the question to its basic assumptions, then turn those assumptions into statements. Once that is accomplished, you can apply ITTIL to the resulting statements.

Turning questions into statements is sometimes easy, but at other times it requires deeper introspection.

Let us start with an easy one.

Question: "Why is my dog aggressive?"

In order to convert this to a statement, look at the underlying assumption.

That's an easy one: "My dog is aggressive."

All you have to do then is apply the ITTIL technique on this statement. If the untrue statement that your dog is aggressive proves useful to you at the moment, then what to do will become obvious. You might do some research and find that your dog simply lacks exercise. You might take the dog to the vet, or even a pet psychologist. There doesn't need to be a story or drama surrounding the action you take. No guilt or suffering surrounding the belief that your dog is aggressive, because you don't believe it—you're simply using the untrue thought in the moment.

Now for another question that is slightly more involved: "Why is life so unfair to me?"

This subjective question is full of assumptions. To name just a couple, it assumes life is capable of being fair or unfair, as if it's an entity with human characteristics and moral judgments. "To me," seems to imply that life discriminates by being unfair to "me" but perhaps not to others.

The assumptions just noted would be made into the following statements:

- Life is capable of being fair or unfair.
- Life is unfair to me but not to others.

Now for an even trickier question.

Let us say that what is of primary importance to a person is having her wedding in a certain small church with a small venue for the reception.

In this case, the question "Should I have a small wedding or a large one with many guests?" would probably never even arise. It wouldn't arise because we don't usually ask ourselves questions when we're perfectly clear about the answers.

Let's make this situation a little more realistic and say there is no primary importance being given to a small church with a small reception. Let us also say that this question brings up feelings of anxiety.

"Should I have a small or a large wedding?" now carries a lot of potential underlying thoughts.

Why is the question asked in the first place? What's behind the question?

Breaking it down, what are the priorities? Is it money? Having fun?

Why would the idea of having a small wedding arise?

Why would the idea of having a large wedding arise?

What difference does having a small wedding versus a large one make? *Bingo.*

That last question hits home, and you know this because your anxiety meter is rising.

You can use the "I AM THINKING . . ." technique for all the replies that come to you.

It might look something like this:

"**I AM THINKING** . . . a large wedding would make my friends and relatives happy."

"**I AM THINKING** . . . a large wedding would mean that I wouldn't be disappointing anyone."

"**I AM THINKING** . . . a large wedding would impress people and I'd have photos of everyone who attended."

"**I AM THINKING** . . . I'm affected by the opinions of others."

"**I AM THINKING** . . . a small wedding would be more intimate."

"**I AM THINKING** . . . a small wedding would be easier and more affordable."

"**I AM THINKING** . . . a small wedding would mean that many people would not be invited."

"I AM THINKING . . . a small wedding would mean I'd have to explain myself to people who were not invited."

"I AM THINKING . . . what people think about me is important."

"I AM THINKING . . . I want people to like me."

This one question was loaded with statements because there was a lot going on behind the scenes that prompted the thought. Breaking down the question into the statements that caused it to arise in the first place allows you to apply the ITTIL technique to each belief.

With belief gone, it is now possible to approach the question with newfound clarity. You are aware of what you want, and you are also aware of why you want what you think you want. From there, you simply choose the untrue statement that is the most beneficial at the moment.

Finally, let's explore a practical question based on a seeking thought (what is being sought here is an explanation for a belief held as a fact): "Why is the universe expanding?"

First of all, the word "the" seems to assume that there is just one universe.

Second, the question assumes that the universe is expanding.

Third, it assumes that the universe has boundaries.

Finally, it assumes that the boundaries consist of observable energy.

These noted assumptions would be made into the following statements:

- There is only one universe.
- The universe is expanding.
- The universe has boundaries.
- These boundaries consist of observable energy.

With a question converted into statements in the manner described, applying ITTIL is easy, though this case involves seeking thoughts (what is being sought is an explanation), which is covered in the next chapter on advanced applications of the ITTIL technique.

A QUESTION OF BENEFIT

When belief is removed from the equation, thoughts lose their heaviness. They stop becoming good or bad, positive or negative. Without belief, thoughts are either of value at the moment or not.

But how is value determined?

Something beneficial can be of practical value or it can simply be something fun, pleasant, or relaxing.

How is this determination made?

That depends on you. Everyone is different. What is of value to one person is not necessarily of value to another.

Let's say I have the thought, "I'd love to go to a movie."

This thought doesn't have practical benefit in the sense that it doesn't provide an income (it actually costs money), and it takes around two hours of valuable time during which I could be writing or practicing the piano. But a thought doesn't need to have practical value for it to be beneficial. Fun is valuable to me! So, thoughts that are fun or that promise fun activities can be beneficial.

What is beneficial depends on the situation. If I want to hand over a draft to my editor tomorrow and feel I'll need every free moment of the day to finish my manuscript, the thought, "I'd love to go to a movie," while fun, would probably not be deemed beneficial at the moment!

Thoughts that allow the space for love, happiness, or peace are of value to me.

After ITTIL, I often found myself quite surprised at what thoughts I'd begun to find beneficial. Thoughts that I used to believe were negative I no longer saw that way, and on some occasions, I'd find myself deciding to use them.

A good example is the story behind what I once considered to be a negative thought: "I'm too fat!"

It all started shortly after my twenty-sixth birthday, when something really odd happened. If I were to eat two entire pizzas in one day and empty a carton or three of Häagen-Dazs, and perhaps wipe clean a family-size bowl of tortellini with marinara sauce and a ton of cheese, I started noticing the definition in my stomach muscles blurring into obscurity. Strange, right?

It took a couple of years for my muscle definition to give way to a thin, discernible layer of fat, but for me, it felt like the end of the world.

See, I was told that I'd *never* get fat. That it just wasn't in my makeup. I used to believe that I couldn't get fat like I believed any other "fact" I'd been taught in physics or chemistry class, and so I continued eating as though I were still a teenager.

Then I hit the big three-oh. Now when I wore a tight T-shirt, the tummy fat was actually visible.

When I was thirty-one, the sister of the owner of the airline I was working for said, "You'd better watch that nice, slim body of yours or it won't be nice or slim for very long."

Suddenly, I became self-conscious in a way that I'd never thought possible before.

I could get fat!

I'd believed that I couldn't, and now I had another person saying that I could. Somebody had noticed, and I could no longer deny what I was seeing in the mirror.

I was married and my wife wasn't in the least concerned about my weight (if anything, she believed I was underweight), so it wasn't as if I were on the market, trying to attract women or anything. And yet I still felt miserable.

Probably because I had this idea of myself and how others viewed me, and now since I could be fat, I could be anything: an idiot, lazy, old, you name it, the list was endless.

So when the thought, "I'm too fat!" arose, I believed it and I felt that I had to do something about it.

For years, I put myself through the yo-yo diet:

- Dieting like Gandhi for a few weeks, thereby regaining my silhouette for a few months.
- Falling back into the old belief that I was impervious to getting fat.
- Eating like a teenager.
- Thinking, "I'm too fat!" and starting the whole process all over again.

Because I believed the thought that said, "I'm too fat!" I wasn't using it, *I was allowing myself to be used by it!*

I was miserable every time I believed I was too fat. When I was thin again, I'd believe I'd stay that way forever, and that I'd dieted for the last time. That I would never again do something to put myself though the experience of being too fat. But I'd eventually betray myself, and thus my beliefs about myself, taking my self-esteem along with them.

Fast-forward to when I started using the ITTIL technique.

At that point, when the thought, "I'm too fat," arose, I knew it was not true. I didn't believe the thought, because I knew the opposite thought, "I'm not too fat," was also not true.

And since it wasn't true, it also wasn't seen as negative. It was simply a thought.

But where did that leave me?

With three choices:

1. I could use the original thought, "I'm too fat."
2. I could use the opposite thought, "I'm not too fat."
3. I could determine that neither thought was beneficial at the moment and drop them both.

How I used the thought would depend on the situation.

If I was in a restaurant, about to order, I could use the original untrue thought, "I'm too fat," and pick out something that wouldn't exceed my calorie intake limit for the day.

If I was at a social gathering, I might use the equally untrue opposite thought, "I'm not too fat," so that I could feel good about myself and project that feeling in my self-confidence through my positive self-esteem.

If I was going for my FAA physical and stepping on the scale, the thought, "I'm not too fat," would be of more benefit to me since I couldn't do anything about my weight at that moment other than accept it as it was.

At earlier stages of the practice of the ITTIL technique, there were times I felt the need to find some reasoning in order to see both the original and the opposite thought as equally untrue.

So in the case of the FAA physical or the social gathering, my reasoning might be "I'm not too fat, because I'm always exactly the way I need to be in the moment."

If the reasoning that supported the opposite thought was rekindling belief, I'd revisit the original thought, "I'm too fat," and use reasoning to support it, so that I could neutralize the belief in the opposite thought that I was not too fat.

My reasoning would include telling myself I'm too fat because my belt is straining and the collar of my shirt is cutting into my neck. Or simply that I didn't feel great like I used to—I felt heavier and running seemed harder.

If I'd find myself believing the original thought all over again, I'd swing the pendulum the other way to find a neutral, belief-free balance.

This neutral, belief-free point is where supporting reasoning is no longer needed, since both thoughts are seen as equally untrue.

I've given examples of where the original thought could be beneficial and where the opposite thought could also be beneficial. What about the instance where neither thought is beneficial?

Let's say I'm in bed, about to sleep, and the thought, "I'm too fat" arises. I would determine that the thought and its opposite are both not beneficial at the moment. Why?

Well, because I'm in the business of going to sleep right now. Bring on thoughts of sheep hopping over fences, thank you very much!

Determining the benefit of a thought is a personal thing. There's no right or wrong in choosing to use or discard a thought. There's no belief to create regret.

Once you've come to the point where you don't believe the thought or its opposite, determining if a thought is beneficial is the easiest part of the ITTIL technique.

Experience will be your teacher, and soon even determining the benefit of a thought will be as obvious as it is automatic.

It becomes like using your hands. When they are beneficial, you use them. It's automatic. You don't sit there and philosophize, "Am I my hands? If so, what happens when I'm not aware of my hands, do I still have hands? If I really don't have hands, how can I use them? If I do have hands, then hands are a part of me, so if I lose my hands, is there less of me?"

This inquiry seems utterly nonsensical. Hands are considered a tool and they are used that way.

We are conditioned to identify with our thoughts and to believe them to be true, however it doesn't have to be this way. There is no need for the suffering that is associated with believing your thoughts.

When thoughts are used as a tool, the way our hands are, then there is a great freedom. A weight is lifted.

CHANGING EVERYTHING

Once you have finished with the fulfillment actions in this chapter, you will be equipped to put belief to an instant end, one thought at a time, one moment at a time.

With the ITTIL technique, you can dismantle your belief the moment it arises. In order for this to occur, of course, the technique has to be practiced. This might seem obvious, but it is as easy to do as it is easy not to do.

It is important to understand that there is no belief that is of more or less consequence than any other. A belief is a belief. All belief must end for suffering to end, not just some beliefs, or only the really deep-rooted ones. Give as much attention to the thought that says, "This is going to be a lousy day," as you would a deeply rooted thought that says, "Death is a certainty for all of us." Just because thousands, millions, or even billions of people say a thought is true, does not make it so.

Remember that the ITTIL technique is not a philosophy. See it for what it is: a technique. Practice the technique, and thoughts will no longer have that sticky Velcro quality to them. You will find yourself stepping away from your thinking and seeing all thoughts as equally untrue and as wonderful potential tools at your service.

With ITTIL, you will have nothing to fear, nothing to worry about, and no reason to suffer. Anger, fear, anxiety, sadness, depression, shame, guilt—all these are based on thoughts you are believing.

You will find yourself in conflict with nothing and open to everything.

FULFILLMENT ACTION: APPLYING THE ITTIL TECHNIQUE

Negative Psychological Thoughts That You Can Immediately Identify

When you first start practicing the ITTIL technique, try it on thoughts that are making you feel some degree of unpleasantness. It could range in suffering from subtle irritability and impatience all the way to depression, anger, shame, guilt, or other such powerful emotions.

If you're not experiencing any noticeable suffering, sit quietly for a while and recall a time when you were.

Look for a feeling for which *the associated belief is very clear to you.*

Try this fulfillment action on three different thoughts from the past that make you feel a negative emotion.

The examples given are to provide you with an idea of what this fulfillment action might look like, not to imply they might resonate with you. When doing the fulfillment action, come up with your own situations and feelings and thoughts you were believing. Then apply the ITTIL technique to those thoughts.

EXAMPLE 1

Situation: A telemarketer has called your cell phone twice and the third time you were right in the middle of a life-changing conversation.

Feeling: Anger.

Thought you are believing: "This telemarketer should be punished for ruining my conversation."

APPLYING THE ITTIL TECHNIQUE

STEP ONE: Find the thought opposite to the one you are believing.

- "This telemarketer should *not* be punished for ruining my conversation."

STEP TWO: Use the opposite thought along with reasoning to negate the original thought, and stop when both thoughts are seen as *equally untrue.* (In order for this to be effective, it is essential to use *convincing* reasoning that *resonates for you.*)

It took me all of three seconds to answer the phone and hang up on that telemarketer. If I let myself become engaged in thinking about getting revenge, I could miss out on finding a way to get this conversation back on track. Even if I were willing to give up on this conversation and decided on pursuing revenge, what exactly would that revenge entail? Would the gargantuan task of tracking down this particular telemarketer (at this point, I'm thinking detective fees) be worth whatever I'm planning on doing to that person? Is all this even worth another thought on the subject? Hell no!

STEP THREE: Determine if and how either thought could be beneficial to you at this moment.

- "This telemarketer should be punished for ruining my conversation." Not true.
- "This telemarketer should *not* be punished for ruining my conversation." Not true.

Of the two untrue thoughts, "This telemarketer should *not* be punished for ruining my conversation" is clearly the most beneficial as it gives me the opportunity to reengage in the conversation, this time without the anger associated with a belief in a fantasy of revenge.

Note: It might be that you're feeling the temptation to believe the statement "This telemarketer should not be punished for ruining my conversation." Remember, if you believe that statement, then you are bonded to the reverse statement as well (bonded by your resistance to it), and you will not be free of its hold on you. Your new story will be supported by the reasoning you deployed in order to oppose the original thought. At the very least, you'll be carrying the story with you, and your focus will not be where it was prior to the call. Remember, the key to the ITTIL technique is to render both thoughts equally untrue. Keep your attention on this, because it is crucial to the practice of ITTIL.

EXAMPLE 2

Situation: You take your pet to the vet and receive bad news. The vet says that the diagnosis is grim and the only procedure he can recommend will cost $2,000.

Feeling: Guilt.

Thought you are believing: "I can't afford to save my pet, but if I don't do something, it'll clearly be my fault if something bad happens."

Breaking this down to two thoughts gives:

- "I can't afford to save my pet."
- "If I don't do something, it'll clearly be my fault if something bad happens."

APPLYING THE ITTIL TECHNIQUE

STEP ONE: Find the thought opposite to the one you are believing.

- "I can't *not* afford to save my pet."

STEP TWO: Use the opposite thought along with reasoning to negate the original thought, and stop when both thoughts are seen as *equally untrue.* (In order for this to be effective, it is essential to use *convincing* reasoning that *resonates for you.*)

If it were my own life on the line, I'd find a way to pay for it, so saying I can't afford it just means I'm not willing to do what it takes to pay for it.

STEP THREE: Determine if and how either thought could be beneficial to you at this moment.

- "I can't afford to save my pet." Not true.
- "I can't *not* afford to save my pet." Not true.

Of the two, "I can't *not* afford to save my pet" is the most beneficial because I want to save my pet.

Second thought: "If I don't do something, it'll clearly be my fault if something bad happens."

STEP ONE: Find the thought opposite to the one you are believing.
- "If I don't *not* do something, it'll clearly not be my fault if something bad happens."

STEP TWO: Use the opposite thought along with reasoning to negate the original thought, and stop when both thoughts are seen as *equally untrue.* (In order for this to be effective, it is essential to use *convincing* reasoning that *resonates for you.*)

Actually doing something could make it more my fault if something bad happens. If the procedure goes wrong, my pet could die immediately, and since I did something (pay for the procedure) it would be my fault! In other words, by not doing something, my pet could potentially live longer!

STEP THREE: Determine if and how either thought could be beneficial to you at this moment.
- "If I don't do something, it'll clearly be my fault if something bad happens." Not true.
- "If I don't *not* do something, it'll clearly *not* be my fault if something bad happens." Not true.

Of the two, "If I don't do something, it'll clearly be my fault if something bad happens" is the most beneficial untrue thought because I really want to save my pet. Now I can do so without the belief and thus be spared the guilt trip regardless of what happens. Action minus the story. How freeing.

EXAMPLE 3

Situation: You receive a delinquent payment notice with a fine and a threat for a bill you know you've paid. You have a very busy day planned and you know taking care of this problem will take the better part of an hour, getting past the robot secretary that claims it can help you and won't let you speak to a real person until you have wasted twenty minutes pressing buttons and yelling, *"Representative!"* into your phone. Then when you finally do speak with someone, they'll make it sound like they're doing you a favor to fix their company's screw-up and they'll ask you to commit to wasting even more time answering a stupid survey saying how satisfied you were with the service.

Feeling: Frustration.

Thought you are believing: "The company should pay for all this precious time I wasted clearing up a problem they created."

APPLYING THE ITTIL TECHNIQUE

STEP ONE: Find the thought opposite to the one you are believing.

- "The company should *not* pay for all this precious time I wasted clearing up a problem they created."

STEP TWO: Use the opposite thought along with reasoning to negate the original thought, and stop when both thoughts are seen as *equally untrue.* (In order for this to be effective, it is essential to use *convincing* reasoning that *resonates for you.*)

The process of paying me for the time I wasted would waste even more of my time, and if I tried getting my money back for that, the ordeal would waste more time still. I would never be able to balance the time spent with any compensation I could hope to get from them. Just thinking about all this is wasting my time!

STEP THREE: Determine if and how either thought could be beneficial to you at this moment.

- "The company should pay for all this precious time I wasted clearing up a problem they created." Not true.
- "The company should *not* pay for all this precious time I wasted clearing up a problem they created." Not true.

Of the two untrue thoughts, "The company should *not* pay for all this precious time I wasted clearing up a problem they created" is the most beneficial, because this way I won't be throwing away more of my precious time in the hopeless prospect of gaining adequate compensation.

Negative Psychological Thoughts That You Cannot Immediately Identify

Once you have accomplished this fulfillment action, repeat it three more times, but this time for a negative feeling for which the associated thought is *not* obvious and requires the "I AM THINKING . . ." technique.

EXAMPLE 1

Situation: You wake up to the alarm, go through your morning routine like a zombie, and when you leave the house, it is still dark and cold outside.

Feeling: Depression.

The feeling seems to arise for no reason.

Time for the "I AM THINKING . . ." technique.

"I AM THINKING . . . It's dark and cold."

And that means?

"I AM THINKING . . . I'd rather be in bed. Why am I doing this?"

"I AM THINKING . . . Why am I doing this?"

"I AM THINKING . . . my life sucks."

"**I AM THINKING** . . . I'm accomplishing nothing with my life."

"**I AM THINKING** . . . my life has no purpose."

The last one really hits home and as you repeat that thought to yourself, the depression grows in intensity.

Thought you are believing: "My life has no purpose."

APPLYING THE ITTIL TECHNIQUE

STEP ONE: Find the thought opposite to the one you are believing.

- "My life does *not* have no purpose."

STEP TWO: Use the opposite thought along with reasoning to negate the original thought, and stop when both thoughts are seen as *equally untrue*. (In order for this to be effective, it is essential to use *convincing* reasoning that *resonates for you*.)

My life has a purpose. Waking up, getting ready, going to work. Right now, my purpose is dispelling my belief that my life has no purpose. My purpose is whatever I'm doing at this moment.

STEP THREE: Determine if and how either thought could be beneficial to you at this moment.

- "My life has no purpose." Not true.
- "My life does *not* have no purpose." Not true.

Of the two untrue thoughts, "My life does *not* have no purpose" is the most beneficial. That way I can do what I'm doing without a story about a purpose and a belief that I should have a purpose in the first place. Action without suffering. What a relief.

EXAMPLE 2

Situation: You are having a conversation with someone and it seems that there's nothing you can do to get through to them. You try your best to get your message across, but the other person is stuck talking about their take on the situation. You tell the person you understand what they're saying (after all, they've repeated it four times and in four different ways) and you try to get them to hear your perspective, but nothing works.

Feelings: A sad frustration. A sense of hopelessness.

The feeling seems to arise for no reason.

Time for the "I AM THINKING . . ." technique.

"I AM THINKING . . . she's not being logical or fair."

"I AM THINKING . . . her point is shortsighted."

"I AM THINKING . . . she only cares about her perspective, not mine.

"I AM THINKING . . . I have acknowledged what she's said, but she won't do the same for me."

And that means?

"I AM THINKING . . . she's not listening to me."

And that means?

"I AM THINKING . . . she doesn't respect me."

The last one hits an emotional chord.

Thought you are believing: "She doesn't respect me."

APPLYING THE ITTIL TECHNIQUE

STEP ONE: Find the thought opposite to the one you are believing.
- "She doesn't *not* respect me."

STEP TWO: Use the opposite thought along with reasoning to negate the original thought, and stop when both thoughts are seen as *equally untrue.* (In order for this to be effective, it is essential to use *convincing* reasoning that *resonates for you.*)

She's been trying so hard to convince me of her perspective. Would she bother if she didn't respect me? Would she waste all that time and energy? If she didn't respect me, she wouldn't have been so passionate about getting me to understand where she was coming from. I told her I understood her perspective, but she could tell I didn't really mean what I was saying. If she didn't respect me, she would have pretended I understood and changed the subject to something she didn't care about, regardless of whether I understood her or not.

STEP THREE: Determine if and how either thought could be beneficial to you at this moment.

- "She doesn't respect me." Not true.
- "She doesn't *not* respect me." Not true.

Of the two, neither is beneficial at that moment. Both shift my attention away from really listening. With the belief gone, and the story about respect seen as untrue, the compulsion to be heard is gone, and I can listen free of suffering from frustration and hopelessness.

EXAMPLE 3

Situation: You go out to the movies with a friend. You order popcorn and sodas. The movie is not amazing, but decent. Afterward, you and your friend grab some fast food. At home, still restless and dissatisfied, you binge-watch one of your favorite shows for the third time.

Feelings: Restlessness, depression.

The feeling seems to arise for no reason.

So you apply the "I AM THINKING . . ." technique.

"I AM THINKING . . . that was fun. Kind of."

"I AM THINKING . . . something wasn't fun about it."

"I AM THINKING . . . something in me really didn't want to do those things."

"I AM THINKING . . . something in me wanted to be doing something better."

"I AM THINKING . . . something in me said I should be doing something else."

"I AM THINKING... I should have been doing something more constructive."

The last one hits an emotional chord.

Thought you are believing: "I should have been doing something constructive with my free time."

APPLYING THE ITTIL TECHNIQUE

STEP ONE: Find the thought opposite to the one you are believing.

- "I should *not* have been doing something constructive with my free time."

STEP TWO: Use the opposite thought along with reasoning to negate the original thought, and stop when both thoughts are seen as *equally untrue*. (In order for this to be effective, it is essential to use *convincing* reasoning that *resonates for you*.)

The belief that I should be doing something constructive with my time sucked all the fun out of the activities I normally enjoyed. Who am I to say what is and what isn't constructive? Am I supposed to be constructive 24/7? Seriously, what am I, my own personal taskmaster?

STEP THREE: Determine if and how either thought could be beneficial to you at this moment.

"I should have been doing something constructive with my free time." Not true.

"I should *not* have been doing something constructive with my free time." Not true.

Of the two, "I should *not* have been doing something constructive with my free time" is the most beneficial. This way I can enjoy what I'm doing without the fun-sapping guilt.

MOVING FORWARD WITH
THE ITTIL TECHNIQUE

The ITTIL technique only works when it is applied. Merely doing the fulfillment actions in this book and then applying the ITTIL technique once, twice, three times thereafter won't do the trick.

Apply the ITTIL technique every moment the opportunity arises.

Your diligence in the practice will be quickly rewarded. In as little as a week, the three simple steps will come naturally to you and identifying the thought that you are believing will become second nature. The "I AM THINKING . . ." technique is very powerful and effective at uprooting your underlying thoughts. The more you use this technique, the more aware you will become of your thinking. The distance it provides will make using the ITTIL technique even easier and faster. The two techniques complement each other perfectly.

Remember, first work on the negative psychological thoughts you are believing. When you feel you have a handle on them, then you will be ready for the advanced applications of the ITTIL technique discussed in the next chapter.

How will you know when you're ready?

- When you start noticing you are having fewer and fewer negative thoughts.
- When the negative thoughts that do arise don't seem to have a hold over you anymore.
- When negative thoughts seem to carry less weight, to the point where they don't even seem that negative anymore.
- Finally, and most important, when you start feeling significant relief from suffering.

How long this will take varies from person to person. It will depend on how deeply rooted your negative psychological beliefs are and on how diligently you practice the ITTIL technique.

The beauty of the practice is that in the moment you are freed from a belief after the completion of step two, you are freed from the suffering it brings. That opening is an awakening to the present moment, at which point the thought has the potential of being beneficial with no psychological downside.

TRAUMA AND OTHER MAJOR PSYCHOLOGICAL CHALLENGES

After talking with people all over the world about their experiences since the first edition of this book, I have noticed that the people who have difficulty moving forward with the ITTIL technique at this stage—almost without exception—are all facing some form of past trauma or long-term major psychological challenge.

In these cases, the ITTIL technique on its own is usually not enough to help people break free of these deep wounds and psychological challenges.

If you find yourself in this situation, seek help. You don't have to do this on your own. There are plenty of experts out there that have been specially trained and could be of great benefit to you in dealing with these issues.

6.
Advanced Applications of the ITTIL Technique

WHEN BELIEF DIED

I could hear the ignition firing up the number-two engine, less than a minute after I'd received that email from my brother about my dad.

Out of nowhere, the thought came to me: *Who says he's dead?*

That triggered the ITTIL technique which I'd been practicing for several years by then.

All thoughts are equally untrue.

Having applied the ITTIL technique for some time, and on deep-rooted practical beliefs, I was shocked that I'd so easily believed my brother's words: "Dad died five minutes ago."

Only just before that email, as far as I was aware, Dad was in the hospital, ill, yes, but alive. I was on my way to see him. That was the dad I held in my world at the time. Actually, even that is not accurate. Just prior to the news, I was thinking about how much time I had on this flight, as well as the next thing that needed attention in my novel. I was planning on a making a few changes to the outline and then working systematically from there.

So just five minutes earlier, when Dad was supposedly already dead, I was completely content, looking forward to some productive writing.

Then, I read one sentence and my universe was turned inside out. Why? Because I *believed* it. Out of conditioning, I believed every word. It took me a while to realize I'd actually trained myself for this moment. I'd conditioned myself to respond with shock, anger, denial, and all the stages so clearly laid out by psychologists, because for decades I'd anticipated how I'd react at the news of my father's death, a man for whom I had a love that cannot be put into words.

That conditioning had started years before I learned the ITTIL technique, and I hadn't really paid attention to it since. So when I read the news, the conditioning kicked in before the ITTIL technique had a chance. As my karate sensei once told me: "As you practice, so you do."

I had been practicing believing in my father's death. I'd rehearsed my reaction by playing out stories in my imagination and accepting them as true. Then I just let it all settle there, dormant for years, and when the time came, the grim stories surfaced.

When I saw what was happening—the moment I asked the question, "Who says he's dead?"—ITTIL kicked in.

"Dad is dead." Not true.

"Dad is *not* dead." Not true.

Both were not true, and this was crystal clear to me.

The clarity was instant. No reasoning was needed.

There was also no question which thought was more beneficial at the moment.

I chose the thought that said, "Dad is *not* dead." After all, it was the thought I'd had five minutes earlier, when I was feeling just fine. Once I was believing the thought that said he was dead, however, I was instantly miserable. I could see what that kind of belief would bring: other thoughts.

There was no end to the stories I could have told myself. If I'd believed them, that would have led to tears, and who knows how long I'd have been suffering and mourning.

Here's the important point: the thought, "Dad is dead," when disbelieved, proved beneficial on many occasions (and it still does). It became beneficial when it was needed, exactly because I didn't believe the thought.

The relief I felt in not believing he was dead, and even also not believing he wasn't dead, was visceral. I felt this rush of gratitude and love—an amazement that suddenly everything was so clear. With this understanding of death, the ITTIL technique was complete within me.

Death was just another story.

Sometimes, it can be a beneficial story, but only if not believed—something experience suggested was rare for most people.

With the collapse of the story of death, all other stories crumbled along with it. The ITTIL technique had been working for me before then, but it was more of an effortful process—I still had to regularly use the "I AM THINKING . . ." technique to fish out my thoughts and then use reasoning to see that it wasn't true.

After that email, I simply stopped believing.

Not believing was such a relief. It felt simply fantastic.

Using the Idea of Death

On the way to JFK and then on to Athens, I used the untrue thought that my dad was not dead, and it served me well.

When I arrived in Athens, however, I used the equally untrue thought that my dad *was* dead.

My brother was there. He was clearly grieving, and I respected that.

I'd have been grieving as well, had I believed as he did that my father was dead.

It would not have been beneficial to use the thought that my father wasn't dead at that moment, because I didn't get the sense that it was an appropriate time to open a dialogue on that topic.

For the record, my brother is an unusually open person. It's not that I thought he wouldn't understand, but explaining all this to him did not seem appropriate or even kind in that instance, and so it wasn't beneficial to me. If he'd asked me, I would have explained about using the thought that our father was not dead, but he didn't.

So I continued to use the thought that our father was dead.

I used the thought while I was at his funeral, but because I wasn't *believing* it, I wasn't feeling sad. Instead I had an overwhelming sense of gratitude that was so powerful I had to resist smiling.

It was a formal event and there was a large turnout. It was obvious to me that a smile right then would not have been beneficial, to say the least!

Years before, I'd imagined my father's funeral as being this unbearable event for which I wouldn't have the strength or the will to even attend.

Not only did I go, to my amazement, I loved and cherished every moment.

When people were offering me their condolences, I used the thought, "My father is dead," but I didn't believe it.

I didn't want to put people in an awkward position, which may have been the case had I been using the opposite and equally untrue thought that said, "My father is *not* dead."

Some of the mourners may have believed their words, others may have simply been following tradition and protocol when they said, "I'm sorry for your loss," or "It's a terrible thing. You must be in so much pain."

When I got such comments, I didn't agree with a yes or even a nod. I just said, "Thank you," or when I could get away with it, nothing whatsoever. With people close to me, a hug said it all, bypassing the falsity of thoughts and words.

Being my father's son, because of the circumstances, I had the luxury of not being judged.

So when I stood back for privacy to be alone in this wonderful experience, nobody insisted—at least not for long—that I take the center stage with the rest of the family.

For the burial, I positioned myself at the back of the horde, too far away to see the coffin go into the grave. I was with my great-aunt, who was in her mid-nineties, and whose husband (my beloved uncle) I'd been told had also died not too long before.

We stood together, in silent communion, linked more deeply in our shared love for this great man, my father, than could have been possible through any words, in any language.

I spent a lot of time over the next few days with relatives and friends. Almost without exception, I used the thought that said, "My father is dead." It worked well for me that way, and I managed to be honest without saying that I didn't believe he was dead (or not dead).

I had coffee with my aunt (who is actually younger than I) a few days later. We've been friends since childhood, and conversation always came easily with her. She is a yoga teacher and into Zen, and figuring she'd be receptive, I opened up to her.

During our talk, I used the thought that said, "My father is not dead," and I explained to her that I didn't believe the thought. I explained how I didn't believe the reverse thought either. I told her about how I use thoughts. About ITTIL.

She's always been a great listener, and it was a wonderful conversation.

I also spoke about it with the mother of my friend who died, the one over whose death I felt such lasting sadness and guilt. She has been like a surrogate parent to me, and I could tell her anything, always, and she'd be open and listen.

I told her about my experience, about this book I was writing, *I Think, Therefore I Lie*. We talked at length, and I was elated that she agreed with the manner in which I distinguished between belief and faith. Being that she was an Anglican priest, her perspective was particularly beneficial in that I saw the possibility of religious people being open to the ITTIL technique as well.

Years have gone by since I got that email from my brother in April 2016, and I haven't shed a tear since then, except in joy.

I see my father in my dreams. Sometimes I'm lucid, and I can direct the conversation, sometimes I'm not, and he's just a character in my dream, as am I.

While I dream about him, I do not believe he is dead. He is simply there, at some age (usually in his late forties), being my dad.

I have recordings of our many Skype sessions, so I can also see him on video. He is there, wearing an older body than in my dreams. In these recordings, he is talking to the Skype version of me that appears in a small box on the lower left of my screen.

But I don't need Skype recordings to bring him into my field of experience. I just have to conjure him. There is the thought of him. The image. The sound of his voice, the feel of his hairy arms.

I have heard the objection: "Ah, but that is not real. That is your imagination. And a dream isn't real either."

That is not a beneficial thought, though. Neither is it true. What about thought is real? If it's not true, how can it be real?

The memory of him—is that real?

Conventional thinking would say it is a reflection of a past reality.

I would say there is no such thing as a past or a reality, at which point the ITTIL technique would kick in and I'd see that my statement and its opposite are both not true!

Let's say my father is in front of me and I'm talking to him. That would be said to be more real than my memory of him. Actually, even in his presence, by the time I'm thinking about him, the subject of my thought is already a thing of the past, for in front of me now (a millisecond later) is another image, sound, feeling. A thought can only be of something past. "My father is in front of me" is a thought. It is a thought of the past (even though it may be said to be a very recent past). And the past is a construct—it is not a representation of truth. It is a thought in the moment. And all thoughts are untrue.

I do not believe my father is dead or not dead.

I do not believe my father is alive or was alive, or isn't alive or wasn't alive.

Life and death are just stories.

They have their place, of course, their value, but if these stories are believed, they can be a source of great suffering.

Without the belief, life and death can be used, and they are lighter than air, floating away, causing no pain. With belief, these stories bear down upon the believer with devastating weight.

It wouldn't be helpful for a doctor to use the thought that the body is not dead when there are no signs of physical life and when to the best of his ability as a physician using the knowledge he has from medical science, he has come to the determination that the body is dead.

Also, if the body were in a coma, it wouldn't be beneficial to use the thought that the body is dead. Cremation of a living body, or burying someone alive, is not beneficial in my opinion (and I'm guessing not in yours either).

So although the story of death is not true, the thought of death can be beneficial at times, and when disbelieved, painless as well. Believing in death might be beneficial for a short period of time, say for planning a burial or cremation, but the element of belief will always eventually lead to suffering.

I have had people say it cannot be done: that it's not possible to just use a thought—especially a thought about death—without believing it.

It has been my experience that not only is it possible, it's as wonderful as it is freeing.

WHAT REMAINS

Chapter 5 served as an introduction to the ITTIL technique, but it is just the beginning.

As you advance beyond using the ITTIL technique just on negative psychological thoughts, and you begin using it to end all seeking and, later on, all belief, you might find yourself questioning the technique or the speed of your progress.

Remember, the ITTIL technique always works; as long as you are following the steps, you are awakened in the moment. There is nothing more to aspire to, no need for anything else—anything greater or better.

Aside from applying the ITTIL technique, change will come independently of anything you do.

Apply the technique, as instructed, systematically and diligently, and it will eventually become automatic. However, don't make this a goal, because the moment you do, you turn yourself into a seeker and you have defeated the purpose of the ITTIL technique because you are then believing in an imaginary future where things will be better.

Once the ITTIL technique occurs entirely in the background, because the tendency toward belief is so engrained and conditioned, there are still some beliefs that might slip by, especially in thoughts whose value is never questioned.

For instance, you might find yourself believing that you are free of all belief! Instead of being disappointed to have discovered this, you might be surprised at your delight in revisiting the ITTIL technique and finding an even greater openness within.

For those of you for whom not believing your thoughts is becoming automatic, there can be a tendency to allow belief in certain practical thoughts, simply because they are useful almost every single time they arise. This happens with concepts such as night and day, gravity, friction, momentum, and so on. We use these concepts automatically when we act. They are almost ingrained in our physiology, as in the presumption of gravity and momentum when we jump over something. We use these basic concepts with such frequency, we might end up believing in them without being aware of it.

To this end, make an exercise of going over certain consistently beneficial thoughts to make sure there isn't a part of you that believes they are true. This isn't to say you should disregard their value—not at all—but an insidious belief, even in something as innocuous as basic Newtonian principles, can tip the scales in favor of a belief in dualism—that is, a belief that posits oneself as a separate container of consciousness observing an external reality.

When all belief is a thing of the past, seeking comes to an end as well. All suffering evaporates. There is no belief, and thoughts that are not beneficial no longer arise, so the need for ITTIL no longer arises either. When the wound is healed, the Band-Aid becomes superfluous. As a technique, its practice is automatic, instant, or perhaps even nonexistent; there is no way of knowing which, and it won't really matter. It won't arise as a question. It is similar to being in love. You don't find yourself questioning why you're in love; you're too much at one with the experience to let such a question interfere.

LETTING GO OF DEEP-ROOTED BELIEFS

In order for suffering to come to an end, *all* belief must come to an end. It might seem tempting to think that dropping just some beliefs—especially the ones we've covered so far, negative psychological beliefs—is all that is required, but it doesn't work that way.

All belief causes suffering, without exception.

The most practical beliefs, though they seem the most innocuous, can be the most detrimental. The principal core belief is that we are separate containers of consciousness observing an external true reality, and that truth exists, out there, separate and independent from us. This sense of separation is at the center of all our fears and our suffering.

Deep-rooted beliefs are sometimes so close to us, we might not even realize we are believing them.

These dominant beliefs may be psychological in nature. A belief that we are victims of a cruel world, for example. A belief based on negative life experiences. Or the belief can be very basic, such as the one that says science holds the answers to truth, or it could manifest as a belief in some scientific "established fact."

Despite its power, letting go of a belief is only as hard as we decide to make it.

With the ITTIL technique, letting go of a belief, even the most deeply rooted belief, can be as easy as it is instantaneous.

Uprooting these beliefs may require extensive reasoning. That will depend on how powerful your reasoning has to be in order for you to see both the original and opposite thoughts as equally untrue.

There are resources to help you with this, especially in the vast library of information on nonduality, since most deeply rooted beliefs are based on a fundamental belief in separation—also known as duality. (This is an important subject and so there will be a section on it in this chapter.)

The idea that one belief is harder to let go of than another is, in itself, a belief, and like any other belief, it is limiting, and it isn't true, and most important, it isn't beneficial.

APPLYING THE ITTIL TECHNIQUE ON *ALL* PSYCHOLOGICAL THOUGHTS

Using the ITTIL technique on *all* psychological thoughts is of paramount importance, because unless you are free of psychological suffering, without having the presence and openness this would give you, working to dispel practical, highly cohesive beliefs will be far more challenging than necessary. If bypassed, and if psychological beliefs are not thoroughly dissipated, tackling practical thoughts alone will not lead to a lasting release from all belief. This is because, at some point, the psychological thoughts you are still holding on to will return and suffering will arise until you free yourself from believing that thought.

As we have seen in previous chapters, the ITTIL technique is first applied to negative psychological thoughts:

- When you have a recurring thought that you can't seem to shake.
- When you have a thought that's causing anger, fear, anxiety, sadness, depression, shame, or guilt.
- When you have a thought that doesn't feel beneficial.

In short: when you have any thought that you feel is negative.

The advanced application of the ITTIL technique is to apply ITTIL on *all* psychological thoughts, *including* positive ones.

Believing positive thoughts often produces positive feelings. If these positive feelings were permanent, I suppose this book would have a very limited readership.

Positive feelings based on believing positive thoughts are transitory, just like the positive thoughts themselves are transitory.

Therefore, in the long run, positive affirmation will always fail, and the suffering caused by believing any thought, even a positive one, will eventually surface.

The following two examples show both the negative effects of believing a positive psychological thought and how the ITTIL technique would be applied in each case.

For the first example, we'll revisit a story from chapter 3.

PUBLIC SPEAKING

Summary: I hadn't prepared for a speech I was giving in college, and I ended up drawing a blank.

Positive psychological thought I was believing: "I'm a great speaker."

Feelings: Anger, humiliation.

APPLYING THE ITTIL TECHNIQUE

STEP ONE: Find the thought opposite to the one you are believing.

• "I am *not* a great speaker."

STEP TWO: Use the opposite thought along with reasoning to negate the original thought, and stop when both thoughts are seen as *equally untrue*. (In order for this to be effective, it is essential to use *convincing* reasoning that *resonates for you*.)

Supporting reasoning: That I drew a blank didn't mean I was not a great speaker, but not doing anything about it at the time and consigning myself to a fit of self-loathing did. A great speaker would have improvised—found some way to make a joke out of it. A great speaker would have turned the situation in his favor, using it to connect with the audience. A great speaker might have told a story in order to quickly engage the listeners. And all great speakers usually come prepared, whereas I had not. Most important, great speakers are there to offer something to their listeners, and I was just there to show off my great speaking abilities.

STEP THREE: Determine if and how either thought could be beneficial to you at this moment.
- "I am a great speaker." Not true.
- "I am *not* a great speaker." Not true.

Of the two untrue thoughts, "I am *not* a great speaker" is clearly the beneficial one. Using this thought, I could drop all the silly expectations and be who I was. Maybe I would prepare next time. Whatever I did, there wouldn't be a story around it—no belief to live up to and make me feel miserable. Using the thought, "I am *not* a great speaker," without believing it, I could be in college for the reason I presumably went to college in the first place: to actually learn something.

This next example is more complex, but important. It shows how a positive belief can trigger the opposite negative belief and cause suffering indirectly.

WHERE'S MY MOJO?
Situation: One day, my golden retriever, Mojo, was nowhere to be found. I'd checked the house, the backyard, and a three-block radius from our home. None of the neighbors I'd asked had seen him. Mojo had vanished. After looking for two hours, my wife got on a local

Facebook page for lost animals and I went back home and started printing flyers.

Positive psychological thought I was believing: "There's a good chance of finding Mojo."

Four hours later, I was posting my second batch of flyers and I had the opposite thought: "There's *no* good chance of finding Mojo."

Result: I felt a rising despair. I was conjuring images of a future without our dog. I imagined he'd been stolen, or worse, he was lost, frightened, walking toward the highway. How would the kids react to the news? Our youngest had already gone to sleep, but what would I tell him in the morning?

As I posted another flyer, I wondered if I shouldn't just give up and go back home. It was unlikely anyone would read the flyers until the morning, and by then Mojo would probably have been run over by a car, having suffered a slow, painful death as he bled out, abandoned on the side of the road, alone and terrified for the long minutes he'd struggled to stay alive and—

I woke up to what was happening before I could torture myself much longer with the story I was imagining. I'd believed the thought that I had a good chance of finding our dog, and then so many hours later, doubt kicked in converting me, for a brief while, to the opposite belief, "There's *no* good chance of finding Mojo." When I realized what was happening, I applied the ITTIL technique and dropped my belief that was causing me the suffering. Without the element of belief, I used the thought that said, "There's a good chance of finding Mojo," and I returned home after six hours of searching.

APPLYING THE ITTIL TECHNIQUE

STEP ONE: Find the thought opposite to the one you are believing.
- "There's a good chance of finding Mojo."

In this case, this opposite thought happens to be the positive thought I was believing initially. As circumstances changed (time passed and I still hadn't found Mojo), doubt overpowered me and I'd suddenly shifted belief to the opposite thought: "There's *no* good chance of finding Mojo."

Belief in the positive thought triggered belief in its opposite.

The instructions for the first step are simple and clear: Find the thought opposite to the one you are believing. Since I was currently believing there was no good chance of finding Mojo, the opposite thought becomes the original thought. This might seem confusing, but in practice, it's very easy if you simply remember to always apply the ITTIL technique on whatever thought you are *currently* believing.

If I'd had the presence to catch myself believing the positive thought, "There's a good chance of finding Mojo," before I'd switched beliefs, I could have applied the ITTIL technique to that positive thought and spared myself experiencing any suffering around that story whatsoever.

STEP TWO: Use the opposite thought along with reasoning to negate the original thought, and stop when both thoughts are seen as *equally untrue*. (In order for this to be effective, it is essential to use *convincing* reasoning that *resonates for you*.)

Supporting reasoning: Mojo wasn't a missing child, or a cute and helpless puppy, and so the axiom that every passing hour spells impending doom didn't apply in this case. He was a very friendly old dog and it was likely that some family had taken him into their home temporarily until they could locate Mojo's human.

There were children in this neighborhood, so for the most part, cars drove slowly. Mojo was a big dog, and should have been easy to spot, assuming the car had its headlights on.

STEP THREE: Determine if and how either thought could be beneficial to you at this moment.

- "There's a good chance of finding Mojo," Not true.
- "There's *no* good chance of finding Mojo." Not true.

Using the thought, "There's a good chance of finding Mojo," was the obvious choice. Now, however, without the *belief* in the thought, there was no chance that doubt would cause me to believe in the opposite thought.

Dropping the belief didn't make me feel happy, but the suffering was gone and what was left was a feeling of peace. The horrible stories I'd told myself just moments earlier about what might have happened were gone. What remained was a cool night breeze and the expansive starlit sky above.

I parked the car and was about to go into the house when I thought of one last place to search. Nestled in between our recycling bin and the open gate door was our beloved Mojo, lying in a fetal position. He looked at me with sad eyes, as though he'd been through a terrible fright. I have no idea what he'd experienced, of course, but his timid entrance into our kitchen was quite out of character. He bowed his head and wagged his tail tentatively. It seemed he was grateful to be reunited with his family.

In this story, the original belief I held, that there was a good chance of finding Mojo, most would consider a positive belief. Admittedly, it wasn't extremely positive—my wife had the market cornered on that, saying we were *definitely* going to find him—but it was positive nonetheless.

This is a good example of how even a presumably positive thought, if believed, can cause suffering. If the experience does not match the belief, whether the belief is perceived as positive or not, there is suffering. After six hours, I hadn't found Mojo. The belief was that there was a good chance I would find our dog, but the situation was that six hours had gone by and I still hadn't found him. Believing that the longer time passes, the lesser the chances were of finding our furry friend, led to doubt. This doubt created an internal conflict in which I shifted belief to the opposite thought. That triggered a negative feeling, which served to wake me up in order to apply the ITTIL technique and thereby end my suffering.

For the final examples, the ITTIL technique will be applied on three simple thoughts that arise in clearly practical situations but are psychological in nature. When reading these stories, try to imagine yourself in a similar situation you can relate to, and imagine you're believing the thought. Find the associated feeling that comes with the thought.

EXAMPLE 1

Situation: You see a doctor about a chronic condition that has been troubling you. The doctor recommends a course of action but doesn't sound confident about your chances of getting better. He says the procedure will have a 40 percent success rate if done immediately, and a 25 percent success rate if you wait for more than a month.

You get a second opinion. This doctor recommends the same procedure but says if you do it within the next seventy-two hours, you'll have a 65 percent chance of getting better, and if you wait a month, chances are 25 percent the procedure will work. He adds another statistic to reinforce his point, stating that 30 percent of those who delayed taking action for three months never recovered.

Hoping for some consistency, you go to a third doctor, who comes highly recommended by a friend and has top reviews on several websites. This doctor recommends a procedure you've never heard of and doesn't offer any statistics on it, but otherwise, he agrees with what the second doctor had said.

Feeling: Fear—a sense of losing control.

Practical thought you are believing: "I have no control over my fate."

APPLYING THE ITTIL TECHNIQUE

STEP ONE: Find the thought opposite to the one you are believing.
- "I do *not* have no control over my fate."

STEP TWO: Use the opposite thought along with reasoning to negate the original thought, and stop when both thoughts are seen as *equally untrue.* (In order for this to be effective, it is essential to use *convincing* reasoning that *resonates for you.*)

Supporting reasoning: I don't have control over what I'll be thinking in the next thirty seconds, so how can I expect to have control over my fate?

The definition of the word *fate* is: "The development of events beyond a person's control." Therefore, if I were to have control over it, it wouldn't be fate!

"That there is even such a thing as fate has an opposite," which is, "There is *no* such thing as fate." Therefore, by definition elimination, the statement that there is such a thing as fate is not true.

The assumption in the original statement is that not only is there such a thing as fate, but fate is something I have. It's *my* fate. This implies a separate fate for me, and a separate one for others. How is the belief in control, let alone in fate, of any use to me?

STEP THREE: Determine if and how either thought could be beneficial to you at this moment.
- "I have no control over my fate." Not true.
- "I do *not* have no control over my fate." Not true.

Of the two untrue statements, "I have no control over my fate" is the most beneficial at the moment. Feeling that I have no control frees me to decide without the weight of responsibility that comes with the story that I have control. Control or no control, both are stories. In this case, the lack of control serves me. I have done all I can, and I find myself no closer to knowing what is best for me. The only problem in this situation is my belief about control. Without the belief in control, I am freed to act without fear.

The control belief is a biggie. I have used both untrue thoughts, each in different situations, each highly beneficial at that particular moment. For instance, in emergencies, I use the untrue thought that I have control and it serves me well for obvious reasons. Believing in control, however, and not just using the idea, creates a lot of suffering and generates long *what-if* stories. Without the belief—using the thought *I have control*—I can be completely focused on the task at hand without the distraction of the stories that come with that fundamental belief.

EXAMPLE 2

Situation: You have two job offers. Both prospective employers require a reply by Monday at the very latest.

Today is Friday.

The first job is in Hawaii and you've always wanted to live there. The pay is not great and neither are the prospects for advancement. You might get a raise in a few years, but the cost of living there is crazy, even with two incomes.

The second job is in Detroit. You don't know anyone there. No friends, no family, and from what you've heard and seen on the internet, the area you would live in doesn't exactly appear to be an ideal place to raise a family. That said, the money is good. Actually, it's insanely good, and so are the prospects. But your husband is a professional windsurfer and according to your research, the winds aren't great in the summer. Who would windsurf in the fall? If your spouse would work at all, chances are he'd be making a lot less. You don't even dare mention the idea of moving to Detroit.

Feelings: Stress, longing, frustration.

Practical thought you are believing: "There seems to be no way to make a decision I won't regret."

APPLYING THE ITTIL TECHNIQUE

STEP ONE: Find the thought opposite to the one you are believing.
- "There *doesn't* seem to be no way to make a decision
  I won't regret."

STEP TWO: Use the opposite thought along with reasoning to negate the original thought, and stop when both thoughts are seen as *equally untrue.* (In order for this to be effective, it is essential to use *convincing* reasoning that *resonates for you.*)

Supporting reasoning: The problem isn't with the decision, it's with regretting the decision. The regret comes with the belief that there is a good and a bad decision to be made, a right choice and a wrong one.

If after I make the decision I keep my attention on the reasons I gave myself for making the decision in the first place, there would be no cause for regret. Conversely, if I do find myself regretting my decision, all I have to do is look at the other options and focus my attention on why I would have regretted making *those* decisions. That way, I'd eventually see that I could find cause to regret whatever I've done, regardless of the decision I make. If I choose regret, I'll always find cause to regret.

STEP THREE: Determine if and how either thought could be beneficial to you at this moment.
- "There seems to be no way to make a decision
  I won't regret." Not true.
- "There *doesn't* seem to be no way to make a decision
  I won't regret." Not true.

Of the two, "There *doesn't* seem to be no way to make a decision I won't regret" is the most beneficial, because then I'm free to make a decision knowing that regret is up to me.

EXAMPLE 3

Situation: For the first time in your life, you suddenly have money to invest. Because you've never been in this situation before, you never gave it much thought. You had a sense you would be responsible with the money—you wouldn't gamble it away or get yourself a flashy car—but you wrongly assumed knowing what to do with the extra money would not only be easy, it would be fun as well.

Now that you actually have the money, you are facing countless confusing options. It isn't fun and it certainly isn't easy. It isn't fun because you really *do* want that flashy car, but you have a family and you feel it is your responsibility to do your best to secure their future. Buying a flashy car may give you happiness for a short while, but you know yourself well enough to appreciate that you wouldn't be able to keep the feeling of guilt at bay. Just thinking about getting that car makes you feel guilty. Now, if you had a ridiculous amount of money, well, that would be different. As things are, however, it's not enough money where you can afford to do the right thing and afford the fun thing as well.

Feelings: Frustration, desire, guilt.

Practical thought you are believing: "I should do the right thing for my family."

This last example is as powerful as it is common. The belief that you should do the right thing resides deep within our conditioning.

APPLYING THE ITTIL TECHNIQUE

STEP ONE: Find the thought opposite to the one you are believing.

- "I should *not* do the right thing for my family."

STEP TWO: Use the opposite thought along with reasoning to negate the original thought, and stop when both thoughts are seen as *equally untrue*. (In order for this to be effective, it is essential to use *convincing* reasoning that *resonates for you*.)

Supporting reasoning: The statement assumes there is such a thing as a right thing to do for my family. How is that so-called right thing determined? According to a belief. It seems that the belief is that I could and should know what the right thing is to do with that extra money.

If I accepted the belief that I should do the right thing, I'm also accepting some kind of magical knowledge of the future. Because while my intentions might be aligned with my belief of doing the right thing, because I don't have control over the universe, the results of my action may lead to what I would believe to be a wrong or even terrible consequence. And with that belief, I would hold myself responsible for that outcome. This falls back into the story of control. How many times have I done what I believed was the right thing and was appalled by the results?

A good example of this is when I tried doing the "right thing" for my oldest son when he was in his late teens. Rather than allowing him to make his own "wrong" decisions, I gave him strong incentives to do the "right thing." Looking back at this, having changed my belief about imposing my values on my children, I then saw *my* actions as being the "wrong" thing. After ITTIL, without the belief, I stopped looking back at my past in terms of right or wrong because that no longer made sense; it wasn't true, and it wasn't of any benefit either.

STEP THREE: Determine if and how either thought could be beneficial to you at this moment.

- "I should do the right thing for my family." Not true.
- "I should *not* do the right thing for my family." Not true.

The question is which thought is beneficial, not which is true. Neither is true. Without the belief, the associated negative feelings, guilt, frustration, and desire, no longer arise.

In this case, neither thought is beneficial, because I don't see any value in a "right" or "wrong." Without these fundamental beliefs, I am free to act without a story. I still probably wouldn't buy the flashy car, but not because it was the wrong thing to do. I'm not feeling a desire for it now—the impulse to buy suddenly lost its allure, and so it's not what I want at this moment.

If I invested the money, I'd probably choose some long-term financial instrument that I wouldn't have to babysit every month, such an S&P 500 fund. Whatever investment I'd choose, there'd be no regret, no second thoughts. However, if at some point the investment were to require my attention, it would get that attention. Action minus the stories. I'd simply be doing what needs to be done. No right or wrong about it. No belief to create suffering.

Here's the game changer: *right and wrong exist in thought only.* Action that transcends thought is never wrong. To use a thought without believing it—to act from that level beyond thought—that is faith-based action.

I'm not referring to faith in the conventional sense of the word, but at some point in the practice, you might come to wonder what's left without belief. What's left without belief is faith.

APPLYING THE ITTIL TECHNIQUE TO END ALL SEEKING

Cartoon by Chloe Archer © 2018

What Are Seeking Thoughts?

A seeking thought is a thought that searches for explanations (how? or why?) to certain ideas believed to be true.

For instance:

- Why do we have to die?
- What happens when we die?
- Is there an afterlife?
- How could God allow bad things to happen?
- Why do some people have to suffer more than others?
- Why are some people enlightened and others are not?

As you can see, each one of these questions is based on at least one assumption believed to be true. These are age-old philosophical questions that don't have any obvious practical use and they seek an explanation to an assumed truth, as though there could be one.

Other questions that fall into the seeking category, but may have more-evident practical use for the questioner, include:

- How can I stop suffering?
- How can I find happiness?
- How can I become enlightened?
- Why have all the paths I've tried gotten me nowhere?
- Which path or technique is right for me?
- How can I know if I'm on the right path?

These questions are also based on at least one assumption believed to be true. After breaking down these questions to their underlying statements and applying the ITTIL technique on each, the questions can still be used if they are deemed beneficial. The answers may be beneficial as well, as long as they are not believed to be true.

There are other questions, useful to the questioner, that seek explanations but are not "seeking thoughts" in the sense that the answers they seek are unquestionably practical. These questions, along with most rhetorical questions, would fall squarely into the category of practical thoughts.

Such questions include:

- What is the minimum and maximum speed limit on highways in Arizona?
- How can I do a cold restart of my new smartphone?
- What is the maximum distance of Jupiter from the sun?
- How do I apply the ITTIL technique to questions such as these?

For all questions of this nature, break them down to the underlying assumed statements and then apply the ITTIL technique on those statements. Using the ITTIL technique on such highly practical thoughts is reserved for the most advanced application of the technique—ending all remaining belief—which comes later in the practice and will be thoroughly explained later on in this chapter.

How Is the ITTIL Technique Used to End Seeking?

It is used on thoughts, and by extension paths or techniques, that seek fulfillment, lasting happiness, enlightenment, truth, or anything considered lacking, sometime in the imaginary future.

The thought that something is lacking in the present moment perpetuates belief in a story of a future.

The ITTIL technique is about awakening now—in the present moment, to what is. It's not about "becoming" anything at some future time.

If you compare the present moment with some belief of what you think it should be, you will always come up wanting. This is one way you perpetuate a future story for yourself.

The future is always a fiction.

The ITTIL technique ends the belief in a future of any kind, allowing thoughts about a future to be beneficial while removing any compulsion that perpetuates a fictional future. This way, they become potentially beneficial thoughts that assist with actions to be taken in the present.

The sense of lack is gone.

Awakening is a choice made right now. It is not some fantasy goal to be had in the future. *For as long as you see awakening in your future, it will never come.* It cannot come, because by definition, the future is never now.

Once you see that awakening only happens now, and that all that needs to be done is to apply the ITTIL technique, seeking collapses.

Every time you use the ITTIL technique, you are awakened from the dream made up of the thoughts you are believing. This awakening ends belief, which ends your suffering now and leaves you with an openness to whatever arises in the present. The continued practice will make this process automatic, at which point there is no turning back.

Awakening is right now and only the veil of belief has made it appear not to be so.

The ITTIL technique puts the responsibility in your lap: You can awaken right now, if that is your wish. Everything available to you is available at this very moment. **With the ITTIL technique, there's no excuse. If you are still seeking, it is because you are essentially deciding to remain a seeker.** *This seeking will continue until the moment you decide to apply the technique and put an end to it once and for all. When you come to see that awakening is now, the whole story of attaining something in the imaginary future collapses, and the story of the seeker collapses with it.*

The ITTIL technique offers awakening in the present moment. It is the only moment where this can happen.

The practice is itself the freeing of belief, and that freedom is awakening to the present.

The goal becomes the practice in the moment, not something to be attained in the future.

In the freedom from belief, you see that there is nothing to seek, for all that you could possibly want—and can only ever be—exists in this present moment.

Use the ITTIL technique to end seeking when:
- You're thinking of using a technique, method, or path that you feel will make you better than what you are right now.
- You're using thought to find some philosophical explanation, spiritual truth, or truth of any kind.

Feelings associated with seeking thoughts:
- Desire
- Longing
- A deep sense of lacking

If you're experiencing any of these feelings, look for the seeking thought you're believing that is triggering them.

EXAMPLE 1

Situation: Someone you revere as a great spiritual leader is holding a course near you. The email you received warns that places are filling up crazy-fast, and this is your last chance to enroll. You can still get that 25 percent discount. Only two rooms left. People are saying this is going to be a great course and a once-in-a-lifetime opportunity for attaining enlightenment.

Feelings: Longing and a sense of urgency.

Thoughts you are believing: "I haven't achieved enlightenment yet; I've only had momentary glimpses. Life is short and getting shorter by the minute, and so I have to do everything I can to become enlightened once and for all. This course will give me the best chance of becoming enlightened."

Let's break down the thoughts into smaller parts:

THOUGHT 1: "I haven't achieved enlightenment yet;
   I've only had momentary glimpses."
THOUGHT 2: "Life is short and getting shorter by the
   minute, and so I have to do everything I can to become
   enlightened once and for all."
THOUGHT 3: "This course will give me the best chance
   of becoming enlightened."

APPLYING THE ITTIL TECHNIQUE

THOUGHT 1: "I haven't achieved enlightenment yet; I've only had momentary glimpses."

STEP ONE: Find the thought opposite to the one you are believing.
- "I haven't *not* achieved enlightenment yet;
  I've only had momentary glimpses."

STEP TWO: Use the opposite thought along with reasoning to negate the original thought, and stop when both thoughts are seen as *equally untrue*. (In order for this to be effective, it is essential to use *convincing* reasoning that *resonates for you*.)

Supporting reasoning: There is an underlying assumption that I know what enlightenment is, or at the very least, I have my own definition for that word. That definition assumes permanence, since I believe I've had "momentary glimpses." These glimpses are not enlightenment, because they are not permanent. Therefore this thought assumes such a thing as permanence, and permanence assumes knowing what the future will bring. Permanence has an opposite: impermanence. Therefore as a concept, permanence is not true.

The statement also assumes enlightenment is something that can be achieved by me. What exactly is this "me" that is being enlightened? Am I my thoughts, my memories? If so, I am impermanent. How can something impermanent achieve anything permanent? What is this permanent enlightenment anyway and how does it differ from momentary glimpses? More important, how can I know until I'm "permanently enlightened"? Who am I to say what enlightenment is if I haven't achieved it? Others may claim to be enlightened, but what do their words mean to me? The thought that says they are enlightened cannot be true, because it has an opposite, so in what way is it even beneficial to me?

STEP THREE: Determine if and how either thought could be beneficial to you at this moment.
- "I haven't achieved enlightenment yet;
  I've only had momentary glimpses." Not true.

- "I haven't *not* achieved enlightenment yet;
  I've only had momentary glimpses." Not true.

Of the two, at this moment, looking at taking this course opportunity, I find the untrue statement "I haven't *not* achieved enlightenment yet, only momentary glimpses" beneficial. Using this thought, there is no urgency to take this course. No longing, no desire. Nothing to be attained or gained by taking this course. And I still might take the course! If I do, though, it would be without expectations. I am content to go and content not to go. All I could ever want I already have.

THOUGHT 2: "Life is short and getting shorter by the minute, and so I have to do everything I can to become enlightened once and for all."

STEP ONE: Find the thought opposite to the one you are believing.

- "Life is *not* short and getting shorter by the minute,
  and so I *don't* have to do everything I can to become
  enlightened once and for all."

STEP TWO: Use the opposite thought along with reasoning to negate the original thought, and stop when both thoughts are seen as *equally untrue*. (In order for this to be effective, it is essential to use *convincing* reasoning that *resonates for you*.)

Supporting reasoning: I've heard the hackneyed "life is short" story since I was a little kid. My Greek grandmother used to love telling me this over and over again. The message she was trying to convey was beneficial, however: *Enjoy yourself now.* That is quite beneficial, because what other time is there to enjoy yourself?!

But that's not the context of the thought, "Life is short and getting shorter by the minute, so I have to do everything I can to become enlightened once and for all." This thought wants enlightenment in the future. What is to be done now is "everything I can," and that doesn't sound like fun or something I would enjoy. It sounds like stress, especially with that imagined time pressure.

The obvious assumption is that life is short. It's given as a fact. What is life, though? Is there such a thing as a life? This is a big subject, and the story of life and death are covered later on in the advanced application of ITTIL to end all remaining belief, so I won't get into it now. Suffice it to say that there's an opposite statement, "There's no such thing as life," and therefore the idea of having a life is as equally untrue as is the idea of *not* having a life!

Finally, there's the belief that I can become enlightened once and for all. In this context, "all" refers to time, which is relative, and therefore not true.

Also, as seen with the first thought, the idea that the "I" or "me" can become enlightened is also not true.

STEP THREE: Determine if and how either thought could be beneficial to you at this moment.
- "Life is short and getting shorter by the minute, and so I have to do everything I can to become enlightened once and for all." Not true.
- "Life is *not* short and getting shorter by the minute, and so I *don't* have to do everything I can to become enlightened once and for all." Not true.

Of the two untrue thoughts, the original thought is the most beneficial, because it's a call to action in the present. This serves as a great example of how belief in the thought undermines the potential benefit of the thought. The action in question is what I'm doing anyway, the ITTIL technique! Freed from the belief, however, there's no story about becoming enlightened once and for all in what I'm doing. No stress, no time pressure, just action now for freedom from suffering and seeking truth and happiness beyond the present moment.

THOUGHT 3: "This course will give me the best chance of becoming enlightened."

STEP ONE: Find the thought opposite to the one you are believing.
  • "This course will *not* give me the best chance
    of becoming enlightened."

STEP TWO: Use the opposite thought along with reasoning to negate the original thought, and stop when both thoughts are seen as *equally untrue.* (In order for this to be effective, it is essential to use *convincing* reasoning that *resonates for you.*)

Supporting reasoning: Becoming enlightened implies permanence, and I'm not interested in chance or even a story of permanence. I'm not interested in an abstract elusive goal such as becoming enlightened because in my experience, I've always doubted whether I've attained it or not. I have been told that when someone becomes enlightened, there is no question about it. No doubt whatsoever. And so any doubt I have about being enlightened I accept as proof that I'm *not* enlightened, and that keeps me perpetually seeking enlightenment.

What I really want is freedom from suffering, as well as freedom from seeking with its associated longing and sense of lack. I want inner peace. I want openness. I want to be unlimited. And I want these things right now. I don't care about the past or the imaginary future. Why would I wait when I have all I need available at this very moment?

With the ITTIL technique, there's awakening to what is now, and so I don't long for that which already is here and now. This awakening in the present offers everything I wanted from the imaginary, ever-elusive goal of becoming enlightened.

In the moment of awakening, there is desire for nothing. Longing for nothing.

There are still goals of course, but there is no desperate longing associated with attaining these goals—just enthusiasm. And because everything is given in this moment, nothing is seen as lacking.

There is a world of difference between enthusiasm and desire. The enthusiasm that arises when using thoughts without believing them offers all the fun of taking a path toward a goal without any of the downside that comes with desire. (More on this in the next example.)

STEP THREE: Determine if and how either thought could be beneficial to you at this moment.

- "This course will give me the best chance of becoming enlightened." Not true.
- "This course will *not* give me the best chance of becoming enlightened." Not true.

Of the two untrue thoughts, "This course will *not* give me the best chance of becoming enlightened" is the most beneficial. I have determined that I'm not interested in abstract goals such as becoming enlightened. What I really want is what I imagine would be the benefits of enlightenment—and this is readily available at every moment by awakening to what is, and for that, I've got the ITTIL technique.

EXAMPLE 2

For this next example, I'm going to use working toward a goal that I believe will make me happy. As you follow, substitute any goal you have tried to attain that you thought would make you happy. It could be winning a tennis or golf tournament, attaining some rank in an organization, getting the promotion you always wanted, buying that special thing that you've desired for years, getting a role in a Hollywood movie, or performing at Carnegie Hall.

Situation: My goal is working for a major airline.

Feelings: Deep longing. Impatience. Desire.

Thought you are believing: "If I could achieve this one goal, I could relax and finally be happy."

STEP ONE: Find the thought opposite to the one you are believing.

- "If I could achieve this one goal, I could *not* relax
  and finally be happy."

STEP TWO: Use the opposite thought along with reasoning to negate the original thought, and stop when both thoughts are seen as *equally untrue*. (In order for this to be effective, it is essential to use *convincing* reasoning that *resonates for you*.)

Supporting reasoning: The biggest assumption here is that achieving the goal will make me relaxed and happy. Implied in the original statement is a lasting happiness. When I think back on times when I used to have this goal, that's what I meant—an enduring happiness, after which I would no longer have to struggle because I'd finally have what I'd wanted.

I have achieved many major goals, and for a brief while, I was indeed relaxed and happy. But it didn't last. The happiness was by no means enduring, and the relaxation even less so.

The need to find lasting happiness and avoid suffering made me pursue another goal, and then another. Therefore, there's no reason to believe that this particular goal would give me lasting happiness.

STEP THREE: Determine if and how either thought could be beneficial to you at this moment.

- "If I could achieve this one goal, I could relax
  and finally be happy." Not true.
- "If I could achieve this one goal, I could *not* relax
  and finally be happy." Not true.

Of the two equally untrue thoughts, "If I could achieve this one goal, I could *not* relax and finally be happy" is the most beneficial.

With this thought, I can use the goal exclusively to direct my action in the present moment. In this way, without belief in a better future, the action along the path to the goal provides all the fulfillment I could want from attaining any goal.

In this manner, without belief, the path and the goal become one and the same and seeking comes to an end.

APPLYING THE ITTIL TECHNIQUE TO END ALL REMAINING BELIEF

Your last beliefs are dropped in this phase of learning and so using ITTIL for this purpose comes primarily in the final stages of the practice. These are the beliefs upon which most people base their identity—the idea of their own separate existence.

To give you an idea of what these beliefs might entail, here's a short list:

1. There's a me with a beginning (birth) and an end (death).
2. I'm made up of a series of past events and future aspirations and hopes that are contained in memory.
3. I have a mind.
4. I have an ego.
5. There's me and there's an external reality out there I'm observing.
6. I can be enlightened.
7. I cannot be enlightened.
8. It is necessary to believe in order to function.

Deep-rooted practical beliefs such as these are all based on a dualistic perspective. A belief in duality. That we are all separate, subjective containers of consciousness, observing an external reality apart from ourselves. (More on duality and nonduality in the next section.)

The deeper the belief, the more powerful the reasoning may need to be in order to dispel it.

Because this is such a deeply rooted belief, the reasoning used to dislodge it is usually quite involved.

You may feel that my reasoning is too complex or too simplistic or in some other way just not adequate for you. The points I offer worked for me—just powerful enough to dispel the original belief, but not so convincing that I would end up converting to the opposite belief.

Whatever reasoning you use, whether it's lengthy or brief, considered convincing by convention or not, *find whatever resonates best for you.*

For this illustration, we'll use the almost universal belief in death. This story of death is one of the most terrifying and painful beliefs of them all.

Situation: Since the time I was first told that I was going to die just like everyone else, I was upset with that story. When I was a kid, I had night terrors in which I tried to imagine what death would be like.

The idea of death plagued me since Bobby Kennedy was shot and my older brother was trying to lay down the "facts of life" as he understood them.

"He's dead."

"What does that mean?" I asked.

I don't remember his exact reply, but I do remember it made no sense to me.

And for good reason. I was free of conditioning. I was a clean slate.

By the time I was six, however, the idea of death seemed real to me. Conditioning had done its work, and I suffered deeply as a result.

I remember asking my dad what happened after death. His reply was, "Nothing."

I asked, "Can you still see?"

"No."

"Can you still feel?"

"No."

"Can you still hear?"

"No."

I was imagining being stuck in a dark coffin. Naturally, my next question was, "For how long?"

"Forever."

That seemed like an awfully long time.

I heard my father's words, and because I was a kid and they came from him, I accepted them. I believed them.

In the ensuing years, typically before going to sleep at night, the thought would come to me: "One day, you will not exist. The person thinking—you—will never ever think again." Since I believed I was my thoughts, it followed that with no living brain to produce thoughts, I'd have no thoughts, and therefore I'd cease to be. The idea of eternal nonexistence came with a visceral terror that shook me to the core. As though I were experiencing a brief glimpse of eternal nothingness.

It seemed like the worst possible thing, so I kept thinking about it, because I figured if I could live in peace with the worst possible thing, then I'd have nothing to fear.

The trick didn't work—I couldn't live in peace believing that I'd come to a finish that entailed never-ending darkness.

As the years passed, however, aside from these rare moments of pre-sleep night terrors, I didn't give death much thought.

That changed, at the age of fifteen, when my friend, Jan, was killed by a freight train.

For two years I punished myself with guilty thoughts.

Thoughts that said I should have immediately tried to get in touch with his parents to confirm that the story was only a rumor. But I hadn't wanted to. I hadn't wanted to hear the truth. And because I'd hidden my head in the sand, I'd missed my friend's funeral.

And there were even more destructive thoughts that corroded my insides, as though each of these were a gulp of boric acid.

They were thoughts that anyone could have told me were untrue, had I not kept them private. Absurd thoughts that held me responsible for Jan's death because I hadn't said goodbye before that summer vacation. I'd created this insane story in my head that if I'd just said goodbye, I could have saved Jan by shifting events along the timeline enough to delay or hasten his arrival at the train tracks by the few seconds that would have spared his young life.

I was punishing myself. Torturing myself with thoughts and then believing them with merciless tenacity, not sharing them with anyone lest my beliefs be challenged.

Mine was an extreme case of grieving. My early childhood introduction to death from my dad's pragmatist's perspective mixed in with all the angst and existential questions that come with being a teenager made for the perfect storm.

However, the fundamental cause of my suffering wasn't that I was a teenager, or that the first story I was told about death was the darkest in the vast library of stories—those were but catalysts—the real cause was that I believed what I was thinking.

For years, I searched for something more pleasant to trade in exchange for my father's death-as-eternal-nothingness belief.

He seemed to find comfort in the idea that life is continued through our progeny and through society. That didn't work for me.

The idea of heaven didn't work either. Nor did the idea of reincarnation.

I created my own counter belief to death-as-eternal-nothingness, by blending happier, more hopeful beliefs, but eventually, I succumbed to doubt and was left with nothing but the raw concept of death, pretty much as my father had described it. To cope, I pushed the thought of death away.

I used addition to cope with my suffering, seeking happiness to drown the fear and suffering caused by my belief in death. This lasted for a couple of decades during which time I worked on building my family and my career as an airline pilot, while at the same time ful-filling my dream of publishing a novel and playing concert-level piano pieces.

While I spent a lifetime trying to create other beliefs to counter my belief in death, it never once occurred to me to question the story of death itself.

Not until approximately the moment I received news that my father had died.

How could I possibly question a belief held by almost everyone who ever walked this earth?

I'm not sure I can answer that question. It simply happened: the thought, "Who says he's dead?" came as all thoughts do, automati-cally, without my control.

An instant later, the ITTIL technique kicked in automatically, and the belief was obliterated before I could take another breath. The same person who instilled the belief in death, in the act of dying himself freed me from that very belief.

What remained was overwhelming love and gratitude.

As I mentioned when I told this story in the beginning of this chapter, no reasoning was required. It was enough to see that I was believing something for ITTIL to take over. It packed all three steps into one explosive punch, knocking the belief out of me once and for all.

So I can think of no better example of applying the ITTIL tech-nique to end all remaining belief than using it to dispel belief in the story of death.

Thought I was believing: "There is such a thing as death."

APPLYING THE ITTIL TECHNIQUE

STEP ONE: Find the thought opposite to the one you are believing.

- "There is *no* such thing as death."

STEP TWO: Use the opposite thought along with reasoning to negate the original thought, and stop when both thoughts are seen as *equally untrue*. (In order for this to be effective, it is essential to use *convincing* reasoning that *resonates for you*.)

Supporting reasoning: While nobody can claim to have proof of what happens after death—there are plenty of theories and beliefs on the subject, religious and otherwise, but no scientific evidence— it seems that almost everyone on this planet believes there is such a thing as death.

Oddly, whereas there is plenty of controversy on the definition of life, there is a general consensus on the definition of death.

Merriam-Webster online dictionary defines it as: "the irreversible cessation of all vital functions especially as indicated by permanent stoppage of the heart, respiration, and brain activity."

Death is considered real because we observe dead bodies meeting the criteria just defined. Death is real because everyone in history who has lived is believed to have died, with the possible exception of Jesus Christ, because if we assume he was resurrected, then he couldn't have died, at least according to the definition given by Merriam-Webster, seeing as how it stipulates permanence.

But we never observe the dead body we believe to be ours. (Near-death experiences of people witnessing their bodies from above on the operating table do not count as observing the dead body we believe to be ours, since a dead body, according to Webster's definition, is only dead if it is irreversibly so.)

We believe in a death we observe indirectly. A physical death we never experience for ourselves. It's always the death of another.

Equating deep sleep, a meditative thoughtless transcendence, or general anesthesia with some kind of experience of death may have a purpose in other forms of inquiry, but sticking with the strict dictionary definition of death, none of these experiences qualify, since death is defined as a permanent cessation of the vital functions of the body.

Memories may also die when the body dies, but since memory can be lost without the body being dead, memories cannot be part of what constitutes life according to this widely accepted definition of death.

What lives and dies is the body. So if we lose our limbs, does that mean we are less alive? If we gain a lot of weight, are we more alive?

No, obviously—a person is either alive or not. The definition of death refers to the cessation of vital functions of the body. That would not be the cardiovascular system, because a person could be on life support (albeit for a short period of time) with an artificial heart pumping blood and artificial lungs providing oxygen to the brain, and that person would still be considered alive.

It would not even necessarily be the brain itself—there are children who have lived for as long as twelve years almost entirely without a brain. They're born with a condition known as anencephaly and have no cerebral hemispheres, which includes the neocortex, which is responsible for cognition. [6]

Perhaps if a person had a brain and then for some reason were to lose all brain function, then medical science might consider that person "dead."

Even seventy hours after an official pronouncement of death, the body still contains individual living cells (most notable and significant of these are stem cells). These cells are considered separate living entities, with their own life and therefore death.

---

6 "Boy Born Without a Brain Dies Aged 12 of Hydranencephaly," *HuffingtonPost*, August 31, 2014, http://www.huffingtonpost .co.uk/2014/08/31/boy-born-without-a-brain-_n_5743844.html.

Medically speaking, there are clearly defined parameters for death, though there aren't any concretely defined, undisputed parameters for life.

Assuming we accept the parameters of death as given in medical science, it is still only a definition of physical death. In order for this to be our death, we must assume that we are the body.

If this is so, if the body dies, we die.

Where exactly are we located in the body? It can't be the entire body. We can't be our big toe, our foot, our hand, or any of our limbs. We're not our heart or our lungs or kidneys or liver either.

That leaves the brain.

Ask most people where they're located in the body, and they'll point to their head, typically to the center of their forehead, indicating their brain.

Leaving the few and extreme cases of anencephaly aside, there are many known instances of people surviving with certain parts of the brain either damaged or missing. Assuming we do need some portion of our brain to survive, then how much is needed to be considered alive?

Since I don't have an answer for this, let's say that we need at least half a brain to be alive. (There is a case of a lady who was born with only one hemisphere of her brain and she is not only alive, she functions well in society.)[7]

If we could sustain this one half of the brain with blood and oxygen, we could then continue to live. Therefore, if no other organs were necessary to support this essential part of the brain, in the sense that they could theoretically be replaced with an artificial substitute, this one half of the brain must constitute both what we are and where we are located in the body.

---

[7] "Girl Born with Half a Brain Is Only Person in World to See Both Fields of Vision Through One Eye," *Daily Mail*, July 21, 2009, http://www .dailymail.co.uk/health/article-1200958/Girl-born-half-brain-person -world-fields-vision-eye.html.

So, are these millions of brain cells, when alive and held together to form the requisite portion of the brain required to maintain our life, responsible for our individual consciousness?

I say "when held together" because if these brain cells were separated and yet kept alive, on their own, they would not constitute a brain and therefore, though the requisite cells were alive, according to this theory, we would not be.

So does the sum of x number of cells, when physically held together, somehow yield individual consciousness—or rather sentience—that makes us alive?

It follows logically that since, together, these brain cells form an individual life and separate they do not, some element or attribute y must exist when the aggregate number of living proximate cells reaches the number x.

What is this y?

Individual, separate consciousness? A shared field of consciousness? A unified field of consciousness? Medical science offers no answer.

Such a fundamental question is dismissed. It is considered out of the domain of medical science and in the realm of religion or philosophy.

This fundamental question remains unanswered by medical science, and yet medical science claims, and completely accepts, the existence of a separate individual human life with a beginning (birth) and an end (death).

It is a huge castle built on nothing at all.

How can science make a claim of a person living or dying when none of the elements of life—and therefore the end of life—can be adequately defined?

Life is said to exist as long as the organism containing life exists. How are these organisms defined?

Specifically, how is a human being defined?

This is an important question, because in order for a human being to be alive—have a life—that organism must meet the definition of a human being.

Most of us believe we are human beings. Most of us also believe we are alive. We think of being alive *as* being human beings.

So when exactly did we become alive as human beings?

If the story of life is true, then it follows that the story of being alive is true. And to be alive, we must meet and maintain the definition of the host organism.

A human being is said to consist of trillions of cells. Each cell is considered a separate organism said to have a life of its own.

So how many cells are required to constitute the beginning of life for a human being?

If a sperm fertilizes an egg, is that fertilized egg—the resulting single-celled organism (zygote)—a human being?

The zygote divides, forming a group of cells referred to as a blastocyst. Do we have a human being yet?

The inner cells of the blastocyst form an embryo. Human yet?

How about when enough cells group together, and it's called a fetus? Is that now a human? No? How about after one month? Two? Three?

Nine months later, when the fetus exits the mother's body, it is said to be born, and is then referred to as an infant.

What about premature babies? With today's technology, they can be born as young as 23 weeks and still survive. In the future, who knows? It is possible that a baby could be conceived and gestate without ever being inside another body.

Since 1500 BCE, babies have been born by cesarean section.

Today, mothers who elect to have cesareans can choose their child's birthday (with certain limits) prior to the baby's due date.

Obviously then, life isn't put into the baby by the act of it being outside the mother, simply because that act is labeled by medical and social convention as "being born." Therefore, clearly, we are living human beings before we're born. But when exactly does it begin?

I used to believe that life starts at the time of conception. This belief is not only supported by the Church but by some scientists as well. That said, there is no scientific consensus on when life begins; and although the Church may decree that it begins at conception (and some scientists allege they have evidence that it does), that does not make it true.

Useful, for some, yes; true, no—not given the ITTIL definition of truth.

The idea that the creation of a zygote during conception constitutes the beginning of life still doesn't make sense unless you accept the premise that life is contained in the living organism. In which case, life is passed on from living organism to living organism as the organism transforms and grows.

The sperm is said to be alive and so is the egg. They both contain life. So the life that the zygote assumes wasn't created, it was transferred. Only the assumed containers of life—the egg and the sperm—changed form. If we accept that theory, the question still remains: where does life actually begin?

Does creation of the right biochemical molecular conditions create life?

It is here that we see the fallacy of even this most basic story: that of an organism having life. If it isn't the actual organism itself that creates the life it is said to contain, then where can a beginning to life be found? And if there is no beginning, there can be no end.

To offer an opposing theory, let's say an organism doesn't contain life, but rather life contains the organism. Or to make it easier: life with no beginning and no end is expressed through the apparent organism, which because it is transitory, isn't real in a true sense.

If life is the energy that animates apparent form, then wouldn't the physics principle that says energy can neither be created nor destroyed apply? If so, life is neither created nor destroyed and it therefore cannot have a beginning or an end. What has a beginning and an end is the apparent form that it assumes, which itself is made out of that very same life energy, in which case the distinction between the two only exists in thought.

What reasoning might support the idea that the organism—the form life is said to assume—is made out of life energy itself? This form, this organism, is made up of cells and those cells are made up of atoms, which in turn are made of subatomic particles, which are basically labels given by scientists for the expression of energy. Therefore the most elementary particles, out of which all apparent organisms are made, are products of energy.

Of course, this idea of life containing the form that expresses it cannot be shown to be true. Nothing can. But it is beneficial in taking apart the belief that an organism contains life. And for the ITTIL technique, that is the sole purpose of using opposing reasoning in the first place.

With no beginning, the life of an individual—the story of a person having a life—cannot be shown to be true. Therefore neither can death.

In order for life to have a definable beginning and end, there must be an external observer who can measure the passage of time and proclaim a thing living or dead. The thing itself cannot proclaim its own presumed beginning or end.

Therefore, the story of having a life with a beginning and an end is only valid from a third-person perspective, and *is neither true nor is it anyone's direct experience. It is not valid from a first-person perspective, which is the only perspective we actually have.*

Did you experience being born? Did you experience not being born and then at some point being born? Did you experience no life, and then life?

Though third-person observations of a beginning and an end to life are clearly relative, and the time in which the observations are made is also relative, they are nevertheless considered a given in the science of biology.

The definition of life fails on the third condition of truth for the purposes of ITTIL: Truth is not relative to anything.

Truth is not relative to time, whereas life, by definition, is.

Truth is not relative to, and doesn't rely on, any assumption, whereas we have seen how life depends on a third-person perspective.

Finally, life is relative to the organism, since the organism is said to exhibit qualities that determine it to be alive. If there is no organism, or organismic state, there is no life. Therefore, life arises as a function of the organism. Since the organism comes and goes, life too comes and goes.

And here we come to the crux of the matter: *The belief that I have a life is founded on the assumption that I am the organism that contains this life.*

If I am this transitory, time-dependent organism, then I fail the definition of truth, and therefore what I hold myself to be is not true.

If I am not true and life depends on me (the organism), then I cannot be alive, and therefore I don't have a life.

If I don't have a life, how can I lose that life? How can I die?

What is there left to sustain the belief in death? Other beliefs.

Therefore, death is nothing more than a belief—it is neither fact nor certainty.

STEP THREE: Determine if and how either thought could be beneficial to you at this moment.

- "There is such a thing as death." Not true.
- "There is *no* such thing as death." Not true.

Both thoughts are beneficial to me, as I demonstrated in the story at the beginning of the chapter. However, in that case, it came in the more specific form of "Dad is dead." The applications of the untrue thoughts, "There is such a thing as death" and "There is no such thing as death," remain basically the same, but instead of them applying to just one person, they apply to death in general.

DUALITY AND NONDUALITY

Dispelling all belief entails uprooting beliefs upon which most people base their identity—the idea of their own separate existence.

Deep-rooted practical beliefs are all based on a dualistic perspective. A belief in duality. That we are all separate, subjective containers of consciousness, observing an external reality apart from ourselves.

The Science & Nonduality website offers the following explanation of nonduality:

> There are many shades of meaning to the word *nonduality*. As an introduction, we might say that nonduality is the philosophical, spiritual, and scientific understanding of non-separation and fundamental oneness.
>
> Our starting point is the statement "we are all one," and this is meant not in some abstract sense, but at the deepest level of existence. Duality, or separation between the observer and the observed, is an illusion that the Eastern mystics have long recognized, and Western science has more recently come to understand through quantum mechanics.
>
> Dualities are usually seen in terms of opposites: Mind/ Matter, Self/Other, Conscious/Unconscious, Illusion/Reality, Quantum/Classical, Wave/Particle, Spiritual/Material, Beginning/End, Male/Female, Living/Dead and Good/Evil. Nonduality is the understanding that identification with common dualisms avoids recognition of a deeper reality. [8]

To finally end the belief in duality, which for most of us is among the very last remnants of *all* belief—I recommend using reasoning that supports nonduality. This is what I used to eliminate the most persistent, difficult-to-refute beliefs of all, before I'd dropped my last remaining belief—the story of life and death.

Using elimination by definition exclusively—in this case, simply saying duality is not true because it has an opposite, nonduality—is

---

8 "Nonduality," Science & Nonduality, https://www.scienceandnonduality .com/about/nonduality, accessed January 13, 2018.

unlikely to pull the plug on fundamental dualistic beliefs, because we've been conditioned to accept almost every concept linked to duality without question since we were little kids.

There is plenty of reasoning supporting nonduality to help disintegrate the resilient beliefs in duality, however. My personal favorites include the Direct Path and the Headless Path.

The Direct Path was taught by Ramana Maharshi and Sri Atmananda.

Modern teachers of this path include Francis Lucille, Rupert Spira, and Greg Goode, to name just a few.

The Direct Path is basically a form of self-inquiry that uses direct experience, without the interference of conditioned thinking, to realize our true nature: pure awareness. All the apparent objects, external (body, plants, trees, houses, mountains), and internal (thought and sentience) all arise in pure awareness. There is nothing discovered in direct-experience inquiry other than witnessing awareness.

The greater majority of people on the planet would claim the existence of objects, both external and internal, as fact. *As truth.*

The Direct Path does not take into consideration this majority opinion, or any conditioned thinking, only direct experience.

However deeply you need to probe into the Direct Path, in terms of applying ITTIL and using this perspective to debunk your belief in duality, it is vital that you do not end up exchanging your belief in duality for a belief in nonduality.

Another approach to nonduality is Douglas Harding's radical Headless Path.

I have found Mr. Harding's writing to be as brilliant as it is humorous. It might not resonate with you, but just the idea that someone can demonstrate so lucidly that he has no head points to a fascinating read and serves as a great tool to crack down on believing . . . well, anything!

Again, there is nothing wrong with nonduality, but believing in *anything* is not the practice of ITTIL.

Duality and nonduality are equally untrue.

Using Direct-Path Inquiry with ITTIL

Let us take the following dualistic thoughts:

1. There are separate, external objects that I perceive.
2. I have a mind.
3. I have an ego.
4. I am my thoughts.
5. There is choice.

1. THERE ARE SEPARATE, EXTERNAL OBJECTS THAT I PERCEIVE

APPLYING THE ITTIL TECHNIQUE

STEP ONE: Find the thought opposite to the one you are believing.

- "There are *no* separate, external objects that I perceive."

STEP TWO: Use the opposite thought along with reasoning to negate the original thought, and stop when both thoughts are seen as *equally untrue*. (In order for this to be effective, it is essential to use *convincing* reasoning that *resonates for you*.)

Using direct-path inquiry as reasoning to support this nondual, opposite statement could yield the following results:

In the first stage of inquiry, it may seem that you see, hear, smell, taste, or touch an apparent separate object.

Probing more deeply, there is nothing seen, only the experience of seeing; no sound heard, only the experience of hearing; nothing that is smelled, only the experience of smelling; no taste, only the experience of tasting, and nothing touched, only the experience of touching.

The seeing, hearing, smelling, tasting, or touching does not arise outside of witnessing awareness.

There is no direct experience of anything other than witnessing awareness.

There is no direct experience of the objective existence of a separate, external object.

STEP THREE: Determine if and how either thought could be beneficial to you at this moment.

- "There are separate, external objects that I perceive."
  Not true.
- "There are *no* separate, external objects that I perceive."
  Not true.

Most of the time, in day-to-day life, I find fundamental practical thoughts useful. This thought is no different. I would say, the untrue thought, "There are separate, external objects that I perceive," is useful the majority of the time.

The equally untrue thought, "There are *no* separate, external objects that I perceive," is helpful if I notice the tendency to confuse utility for validity and therefore start believing the original thought.

2. I HAVE A MIND

APPLYING THE ITTIL TECHNIQUE

STEP ONE: Find the thought opposite to the one you are believing.

- "I *don't* have a mind."

STEP TWO: Use the opposite thought along with reasoning to negate the original thought, and stop when both thoughts are seen as *equally untrue.* (In order for this to be effective, it is essential to use *convincing* reasoning that *resonates for you.*)

Supporting reasoning: Where in direct experience is a mind found? The mind is but a construct. An abstract concept. It has no existence outside the thought that says there is a mind. All that can be found in direct-experience inquiry is the thought of a "mind" arising in witnessing awareness.

STEP THREE: Determine if and how either thought could be beneficial to you at this moment.

- "I have a mind." Not true.
- "I *don't* have a mind." Not true.

This is an interesting one. Most of the time, I find the untrue thought that says "I *don't* have a mind" the most beneficial. This is because the man-made abstraction "mind" has no value to me whatsoever other than to confuse and make other abstract beliefs seem valid. In day-to-day life, I will use the untrue thought, "I have a mind," when someone else uses the word "mind," because I don't find it beneficial to act as though I don't know the meaning of expressions like "What's on your mind?" or terms such as "mind-reading."

3. I HAVE AN EGO

APPLYING THE ITTIL TECHNIQUE

STEP ONE: Find the thought opposite to the one you are believing.

- "I *don't* have an ego."

STEP TWO: Use the opposite thought along with reasoning to negate the original thought, and stop when both thoughts are seen as *equally untrue.* (In order for this to be effective, it is essential to use *convincing* reasoning that *resonates for you.*)

Supporting reasoning: Where in direct experience is an ego found? The ego is but a construct. An abstract concept. It has no existence outside the thought that claims an ego.

All that can be found in direct-experience inquiry is the thought of an "ego" arising in witnessing awareness.

STEP THREE: Determine if and how either thought could be beneficial to you at this moment.

- "I have an ego." Not true.
- "I *don't* have an ego." Not true.

Ego is another man-made construct I don't find beneficial. I don't find any value in the idea of an ego or the many stories that come with it, therefore I hardly ever use the term. I use the untrue statement "I have an ego" when I'm communicating with someone who uses the term, or when I'm reading books that use the word. One such book is *A Course in Miracles* (discussed in chapter 5). While I don't use the term ego, I don't resist it either. I'm open to all words, ideas, and statements; I simply don't believe any of them.

4. I AM MY THOUGHTS

APPLYING THE ITTIL TECHNIQUE

STEP ONE: Find the thought opposite to the one you are believing.

- "I am *not* my thoughts."

STEP TWO: Use the opposite thought along with reasoning to negate the original thought, and stop when both thoughts are seen as *equally untrue*. (In order for this to be effective, it is essential to use *convincing* reasoning that *resonates for you*.)

Using the Direct Path as supporting reasoning: Where in direct experience is a thought found?

It has no discernible location.

More to the point, what is aware of a thought?

Does a thought exist other than as something arising in witnessing awareness?

If the "I" referred to is the subject, then thought is but an object.

However, I am the subject, not the object.

What is the subject to which the object of thought appears, then?

That subject is witnessing awareness.

Deep inquiry shows that nothing can be found other than witnessing awareness itself.

There are no objects in direct experience. Not even thoughts.

Therefore, I am *not* my thoughts.

STEP THREE: Determine if and how either thought could be beneficial to you at this moment.

- "I am my thoughts." Not true.
- "I am *not* my thoughts." Not true.

I'm guessing by now you have a sense of which of the two untrue thoughts I find beneficial most of the time: "I am *not* my thoughts."

I have used "I am my thoughts" in this book only because it was beneficial in illustrating the fallacy of this commonly held belief!

You might object here, thinking that I'm conveniently skipping past the part where I state above: "I am *not* my thoughts. Not true."

If you feel some belief in this statement, or the original statement "I am my thoughts" seems less believable at this point than "I am *not* my thoughts," it is time to use reasoning to find a balance.

This will serve as another example of what to do if instead of seeing both thoughts as equally untrue, your supporting reasoning is so strong that you end up switching beliefs to the opposite thought.

The process is easy. Simply apply the ITTIL technique on the new thought you are believing (in this case the opposite thought).

New thought you are believing: "I am not my thoughts."

STEP ONE: Find the thought opposite to the one you are believing.

- "I am *not* not my thoughts."

STEP TWO: Use the opposite thought along with reasoning to negate the original thought, and stop when both thoughts are seen as *equally untrue*. (In order for this to be effective, it is essential to use *convincing* reasoning that *resonates for you*.)

Supporting reasoning: To debunk the belief that I am not my thoughts:

What is this "I" referred to here?

To paraphrase philosopher David Hume, we are a bundle of sensations and impressions held together in memory.[9]

To this day, many would agree with this definition.

So assuming I am a collection of accrued memories, then without thought, there are no memories and therefore there is no me. Without thought, there is no me who was born and can die. If I were to have an accident and suffer severe brain damage, I would be considered a vegetable and as good as dead. I'd have no memories that could tell me what I am or am not. Without thoughts, there would be no possibility of a me who can be known.

Remember, this reasoning is not truth. It is used only so that "I am not my thoughts" may be seen as equally untrue as "I am my thoughts." This is important, because it is very easy and tempting to latch on to powerful beliefs such as nonduality on the level of thought.

---

9 David Hume, "Of Personal Identity," in *A Treatise of Human Nature* (London: Longmans, Green, and Co., 1739).

When thought is transcended, duality and nonduality become meaningless. Neither has any value. On the level of thought, they both are tremendously beneficial. If believed, however, both cause suffering.

Nonduality has value if it leads to not believing thought or if it leads to transcending thought. As a philosophy, it holds no truth. No words, no matter how beautiful or beneficial, are true.

STEP THREE: Determine if and how either thought could be beneficial to you at this moment.

We went over this before, when we did the ITTIL technique on the original thought "I am my thoughts."

It is useful here to see that though I determined that this original thought "I am my thoughts" was not beneficial (no surprise there), when I did the ITTIL technique on the opposite thought "I am *not* my thoughts," I can see how this thought is beneficial *only* without the element of belief.

If, for instance, I had just done the ITTIL technique on "I am my thoughts" without doing it on "I am *not* my thoughts" as well (so that they were both seen as equally untrue), then using "I am *not* my thoughts" while still believing it to some degree, would result in bonding myself to a new powerful belief. In so doing, I'd be taking a step away from being free of *all* beliefs, and unless I'm free of belief entirely, there will be suffering to some degree.

Nonduality is the most powerful tool to dispel belief in thoughts based on duality. It is *so* powerful, great vigilance is necessary when using it for supporting reasoning with the ITTIL technique. You must make sure you can see both the original and the opposite thoughts as equally untrue and that you don't end up simply switching beliefs.

Here's the main reason why using nonduality needs vigilance: Nonduality on an intellectual level—on the level of thinking—like anything else, like any religion or belief—is not true. However, nonduality can lead to the transcending of thought, just as religion can lead to faith.

If this truth is experienced, it can easily be confused with the thoughts that attempt to describe it. The truth portrayed by nonduality is just as untrue as that described by any religion or philosophy.

5. THERE IS CHOICE

APPLYING THE ITTIL TECHNIQUE

STEP ONE: Find the thought opposite to the one you are believing.
- "There is *no* choice."

STEP TWO: Use the opposite thought along with reasoning to negate the original thought, and stop when both thoughts are seen as *equally untrue.* (In order for this to be effective, it is essential to use *convincing* reasoning that *resonates for you.*)

Using the Direct Path as supporting reasoning: Try making a decision to choose one of three objects that you like in the same category.

It could be three different pieces of jewelry that you like.

Or three different flavors of ice cream that you normally prefer.

Did you directly experience an act of choosing one over the other two objects?

Was there a direct experience of a chooser performing the act of choosing?

If a chooser is found, it is not the direct experience of a chooser, it is but the *naming* of a chooser, and *that is not the choosing itself.* That which names is not the thing itself. It can never be.

Therefore there cannot be a chooser, hence there can be no choice —there can only be a thought that claims choice.

STEP THREE: Determine if and how either thought could be beneficial to you at this moment.

- "There is choice." Not true.
- "There is *no* choice." Not true.

I so love this one. It's typically an even split which of these two untrue statements I find beneficial at the moment. Usually, before a decision, I find "There is choice" to be beneficial. After the decision is made, however, I tend to use "There is *no* choice," and this works just great for me!

Using the Headless Path with ITTIL

Let's try this one simple, basic dualistic belief that says, "I am a person."

APPLYING THE ITTIL TECHNIQUE

STEP ONE: Find the thought opposite to the one you are believing.

- "I am *not* a person."

STEP TWO: Use the opposite thought along with reasoning to negate the original thought, and stop when both thoughts are seen as *equally untrue*. (In order for this to be effective, it is essential to use *convincing* reasoning that *resonates for you*.)

Using the Headless Path as supporting reasoning: I am *not* a person because I only appear to others as a person from a certain distance range.

Move closer and I become a blur. Zoom in more, and cells are observed. Closer still, molecules. Closer, atoms. Even closer than that, particles. And at zero distance, nothing.

Therefore in close observation, I am not a person, I am nothing.

Looking farther away than the normal range, I see a city. Farther still, a country or continent. Even farther, Earth. Farther still, our solar system, and finally our galaxy. Farther than that, countless galaxies, and from an infinite distance, infinity. So from the most distant observation, I am not a person, I am infinity.

Either way, I am only a person from a range of a couple feet to a couple hundred feet.

STEP THREE: Determine if and how either thought could be beneficial to you at this moment.
- "I am a person." Not true.
- "I am *not* a person." Not true.

The untrue statement, "I am a person" can have practical value in day-to-day use, especially when communicating with others; however, as with constructs such as ego and mind, I no longer typically find the thoughts, "I am a person" or "I am *not* a person" beneficial, nor do they arise in my thinking.

BEYOND THOUGHT, BEYOND BELIEF

You have practiced the ITTIL technique on negative psychological thoughts, on deep-rooted psychological thoughts, on all seeking thoughts, and finally on the most resilient practical thoughts believed by almost everyone on this planet.

For a while, following the advanced application of the ITTIL technique, there may have been a need for determining whether a thought is beneficial before releasing it, but that need soon slipped away. You can now see that only your perspective on those thoughts could have considered them as not being beneficial. When thoughts arise, they have some benefit, even if that benefit is in the freedom of letting them go.

The ITTIL technique has become so automatic and natural that for the most part, you hardly even notice it operating in the background.

You have experienced freedom from all belief and now suffering is a thing of the past.

There are no more persistent thoughts. No more recurring, negative thoughts. Thoughts are no longer negative or positive, good or bad.

The running commentary, and the compulsive need to compare and judge, has no benefit for you and no longer arises.

The thoughts that do arise are fewer, and there is no longer a need to demonstrate that they are equally untrue or even to determine their benefit, because that has now become immediately obvious, even in your sleep.

Because thoughts are untrue, they have no weight, no power over you.

You might experience lucid dreaming (dreaming while being aware that you are dreaming), you might not, but either way, no dream has a hold over you once you have awoken from it. No thoughts or illusions can rethread the veil of belief once you have dropped it, because you can no longer delude yourself with thoughts you know to be untrue.

You no longer identify with thought. You no longer claim ownership of thoughts. They are like any object—they simply come and go.

The story of a separate you, who was born, accumulates memories, and will one day die, is now seen as just that: a story. It is a beneficial story that you continue to enjoy and use, but now without any of the pain and suffering that comes with attachment.

Without the story in which to be confined, you are limitless.

Free from belief, you are completely open.

There is no story that desires, no want for anything that isn't already given.

This is awakening now.

So now what?

What happens beyond belief, when there is no suffering or desire?

People who try to imagine this often come up with the image of someone sitting around doing nothing, like a person on some never-ending high.

It doesn't work that way, thank God! While you want for nothing outside the present moment, there is still action.

Enthusiasm replaces desire. You have goals and you plan; only now your plans have no hold over you. They exist only to guide your action in the present.

You might act just as you did before. Freedom from suffering doesn't mean that you drop everything right then and there and become a guru or give up all your earthly possessions and change the world Gandhi-style.

Awakening is not about self-improvement.

Awakening is freedom from suffering and seeking in the present.

There may be some side effects of awakening that can be seen as improvements on your behavior, but they are by no means part of the process. You could be free from suffering and seeking and at the same time still act like a jerk.

The overall personality that you wear as a part of the story of you is not likely to change. Your coworkers and your friends may not notice. Even your family may not see a difference.

It is even possible that *you* may not notice! At least, not at first. This happens when there are no sudden, powerful experiences, and belief is dropped gradually over a period of time until there is nothing left to drop. If you come to freedom from suffering in this manner, a month could go by before you realize that you haven't suffered anxiety, worry, depression, or any of those negative feelings that used to plague you. This can happen because it is easy to disregard what is lost when your attention is no longer on it. If you have a canker sore that has been bothering you for a week, and the pain goes away, you won't realize it until you remember you had it in the first place!

One day, there might be the thought: "Huh, that's interesting, I haven't suffered in . . . months?!" You try to recall something negative and find nothing.

Most people seem to drop belief both gradually, over a period of months or maybe years—during which time suffering slowly recedes—and in powerful, unforgettable bursts that seem to arise out of the blue and result in the dropping of major chunks of belief.

For a handful of people, the shift is explosive. All belief and the suffering it caused is nuked to oblivion in an instant of awakening. These rare instances are characterized by extreme, enduring suffering (usually in the form of suicidal depression) one moment, followed by freedom from suffering the very next. In such cases, the difference is so dramatic, virtually everyone notices.

No matter how freedom from suffering arises—gradually only, gradually and with sudden bursts, or in a single flash—there is often some reactive carryover that lingers for a while.

This might arise as a flare-up of impatience, frustration, even anger or any other short-lived negative emotion.

However these emotions may manifest, they are relatively brief, because there is no belief to sustain them. These feelings come in reaction to certain situations as a result of years and years of conditioning. Depression, grief, and remorse no longer make an appearance, because they're lasting feelings, not reactive conditioned responses.

Whatever negative emotions you experience, they will manifest as reactivity and will appear as a curious surprise. You watch as this happens, apart from it completely, as though you're witnessing a toddler in a restaurant seated at a distant table.

You might think there's a need for the ITTIL technique in such cases. However, unless you feel it is *you* that is being irritable, frustrated, or whatever reactive emotion you're experiencing, and unless you are suffering as a result of that feeling, then there is no need to apply the ITTIL technique. This is because these emotions are merely echoes from the past coming into your present experience out of a momentum generated from years of repeated behaviors.

In time, even these momentary lapses of reactivity will gradually fade away, because there is no belief to sustain them.

At some point, you may find yourself with a great enthusiasm to share and help others alleviate their suffering and their search for truth outside the present moment. With the ever-growing gratitude and love that is your experience now, how could you not?

In my case, the enthusiasm was so great, I stopped writing an almost completed novel for which there was interest from two agents and one publisher in order to write the book you are reading now.

What I've learned over the years is to be gentle and go easy.

The temptation is to tell people right off the bat that belief leads to suffering and the only way to end all suffering is to end all belief. If you do, however, you may encounter strong resistance, and end up turning people off to the one thing you've personally experienced that really works. You may think you can gauge when people are ready, and you may often be correct, but getting this sense about others comes with a lot of experience. Trust me on this one.

I have found that sometimes people ask questions without really wanting an answer—they seem more interested in a debate.

If you see people are trying to start a debate, gently remind them that ITTIL isn't a philosophy, it is a technique and there are other techniques and paths out there that might be more beneficial for their needs at this stage along their path.

Remember, the ITTIL technique is about as radical as they come. It's powerful, and it cuts right to the chase, but I have learned that it isn't for everyone. Some people prefer following a path that is slow and safe. A path where they can continuously test the waters before committing.

For those people you encounter that seem genuinely interested in awakening now, and whose questions have the urgency of an authentic seeker, I still suggest you proceed gradually.

There's an old Greek saying, σπεῦδε βραδέως, which I take to mean *Go slow in order to move fast.* This has been a great tool for me as a pilot and a pianist, and it is also very helpful when it comes to introducing the ITTIL technique to others.

If you want to help, do so one easy step at a time.

There's good reason that the ITTIL technique starts off with eliminating belief in negative psychological thoughts. People accept this with little resistance, because their conditioning is aligned with getting rid of bad things.

Once they experience the tremendous relief that comes with eliminating negative psychological beliefs, they will be open to removing belief in all psychological thoughts, seeking thoughts, and finally all thoughts, even those established as facts.

When helping others, remember how it was for you when you first read this book and started practicing the ITTIL technique.

Enjoy your freedom and the bliss that comes from helping others find theirs.

Your freedom is our freedom.

Thank you from the depths of my heart.

7.

Q&A

QUESTIONS FROM BEGINNERS

Q: I have the thought, "I love my son," so according to you, that's a lie?

A: No. The ITTIL technique is not a philosophy claiming to know what is true and what is not. It is a technique that uses its own definition of truth in order to be effective.

In the beginning, the ITTIL technique is only applied on negative psychological thoughts. Thoughts that give rise to negative emotions, and so unless you have those feelings, you wouldn't be applying the ITTIL technique on such a thought.

Even in advanced applications of the ITTIL technique, the thought, "I love my son," would not be used. It isn't searching for a spiritual or philosophical truth or a path of any kind, and so it clearly isn't using the ITTIL technique to end seeking. And when you find yourself at the point where the ITTIL technique is used for letting go of all remaining belief, it wouldn't apply then either, because the technique is used to dismantle beliefs, and love is not a belief. Whereas belief is sustained by reasoning, love is not.

Q: I believe God exists, and so you're telling me that is a lie?

A: I would not presume to tell you anything. Any statement I could make in the context of ITTIL would, in itself, by definition, be untrue. ITTIL is a technique, not a philosophy. The technique is either beneficial in the moment or it isn't.

Applying ITTIL to "God exists" wouldn't work for negative psychological thoughts, since the thought doesn't bring related suffering. However, if you were using ITTIL to end seeking or to end all remaining belief, applying the technique to "God exists" might be beneficial, and that would depend on how you are using the word "believe."

If you are using the word as defined by ITTIL, you are using reasoning to support your statement, in which case the ITTIL technique would be beneficial.

If the statement comes from faith as the word is defined by ITTIL, then the technique would not be beneficial because any statement made from faith transcends belief-based thought and therefore transcends the need for the ITTIL technique.

Simply put, from the ITTIL perspective, where there is faith, there is no belief, and a thought that arises in faith is automatically seen as beneficial.

Q: I want the ITTIL technique to work, but I have chronic anxiety and it's not taking away my suffering. Am I doing something wrong or is it that the ITTIL technique just doesn't work for everyone?
A: The ITTIL technique was not meant as a tool for therapy, though in some cases it has been used as such. If you are facing a serious psychological issue or trauma, using ITTIL to break through that can ignite a very powerful awakening in the moment. This would require tremendous willpower and determination to unearth the thought that is triggering the suffering—in your case, the anxiety. It would take even more willpower and determination to come up with powerful reasoning that truly resonates with you to negate the original thought.

Some spiritual teachers feel that suffering can be seen as a gateway to major shifts in awareness. This has certainly been my experience.

That said, I am in no way recommending you try using ITTIL, or at least using ITTIL alone, as a means to cure your chronic anxiety.

If you find yourself stuck in a deeply rooted psychological thought that triggers problems such as chronic anxiety—a thought that you cannot seem to refute with reasoning—it might be beneficial to seek help from a psychologist or some expert trained to help you deal with the issue you are facing. Unless you use reasoning that truly resonates for you to refute the original thought, you will just be going through the motions of the ITTIL technique and you won't break free of the belief that is binding you to that thought and the associated suffering it brings.

Q: Okay, so let's say somebody comes to you and tells you they have cancer and they're going to die. If you don't believe anything—and you don't believe they have cancer and you don't believe in death, then how would you even feel any compassion? How can you feel their suffering or care about their situation at all? Would you even care to help?

A: I couldn't ever truly feel anyone else's suffering, though I used to believe I could.

I could create suffering for myself, based on memories of suffering I'd experienced, to make up a story that I imagine matched their suffering. I could suffer, but it wouldn't be their suffering, it would be mine. The result would be two people suffering, not just one. How can I be of help if I'm suffering as well?

That said, I can see that people suffer, but I don't need to believe the story surrounding their suffering to see that they're in pain, and I certainly don't need to create a story to join them in suffering. Free from suffering, free from belief, I'm open. I'm available for them to offer whatever is needed at the moment. If a kid is crossing the street and about to be hit by a car, I would act to save the child, but there would be no story around it. There'd be immediate, focused action. If a kid were lost, I'd help the child find her parents.

Without belief, there is still action to help others when the need arises. There is a deep connection that is beyond thoughts or stories that is not a connection on the level of suffering—you're suffering and I'm suffering; therefore we're connected. I've had superficial connections like that before. It's more of a competition: comparing my suffering to that of the other person. It actually separates more than it connects. It's a cry for attention and it has to do with me, not the other person. Real compassion is nothing like that. It's being available. Really listening and really doing. Doing what is beneficial without a story.

Most of us do this in times of extreme crisis. Sure, there are people who sit back and cry and let themselves get caught up in a story about what horrifying future the present situation will bring. But there are others who in times of crisis drop the story and do exactly what is needed. During those times, there seems to be a natural efficiency of thinking where only beneficial thoughts arise. The urgency of the situation makes it so that there's no time to think up what-if stories, there's just time to act.

Q: What if someone uses the ITTIL technique and decides it's beneficial to him to commit some crime like rape or murder?
A: I've heard many variations of this question.

First of all, the ITTIL technique is not for the mentally ill. Rape and murder are born of suffering, they cause suffering, and they benefit no one.

Any act that causes anyone—including yourself—suffering is not beneficial.

If a person cannot see that, then said person could use psychiatric help and is not psychologically fit to practice the ITTIL technique.

Furthermore, if someone is in a psychological state where he would cause himself or others pain and suffering, he'd likely do it anyway, and wouldn't bother using ITTIL as some kind of twisted justification for his actions.

Q: But if someone doesn't believe in anything, he wouldn't have a moral compass, so doesn't that make the ITTIL technique dangerous?
A: Not at all. Let me explain by talking about morality here, because that's the key to both your questions. When we talk about morality, we're talking about beliefs. A set of beliefs about what behaviors are right or wrong and which personal characteristics or traits are good or bad.

What one person considers good behavior, another person may consider bad behavior.

The same contradicting moral values can arise between different groups, religions, and societies.

So this moral compass you are referring to doesn't point to some true north. It points to the north defined by an individual, a group, a religion, or a society.

In other words, morals are a set of beliefs. The ITTIL technique doesn't latch on to any morals because its basic function is to let go of all belief that arises in the moment without judgment or discrimination of any kind.

Belief is the cause of internal conflict and that internal conflict is what leads to external conflict. War, terrorism, crime, violence of all sorts all stem from thoughts people are believing to be true.

I would challenge you to find a single person that suffers or causes suffering that doesn't believe anything at all while he is suffering or causing suffering.

So yes, if someone doesn't believe anything, that person wouldn't have a moral compass. But the false assumption here is that someone without a moral compass would cause suffering.

Freedom from belief does not and cannot cause suffering because it is belief that causes suffering in the first place!

When the ITTIL technique is applied, belief comes to an end.

Without belief, there simply is no conflict.

Without belief there is no need for a moral compass because there is no suffering and there is no causing of suffering to oneself or to others.

MY STORY

Q: So if no thought is true, then nothing is true, right? Not even you, your body, your history, your future?

A: Yes, indeed.

It feels like you're in an interactive movie.

There can be fun and tears of joy and peace and sleep and dreams. But none of it is real in a true sense. And since there are no degrees of truth, "reality" is just another fiction in which I'm but a character.

As Jaques says in Shakespeare's *As You Like It*:

> *"Life is but a stage,*
> *And all the men and women merely players."*

This may seem that it takes away from life. In a sense, it does—it takes away the element of belief. Without the dark, heavy weight of belief, however, life is lighter, brighter, and free of fear.

Without belief in the story of me, I'm free from trying to really define myself, and free also from all the burdens and limitations I would allow such a definition to impose on me.

DREAMING

Q: Do you dream?

A: Yes, I dream.

Q: Okay, but you say you don't believe anymore. So you don't believe your dreams?

A: Excellent question.

If I'm lucid dreaming, then I'm aware on the level of thought that I'm dreaming and so I don't believe my dreams are real.

If I'm not lucid dreaming, then I don't see a difference between my dream and the waking state; however, I don't believe the dream any more than I believe in the reality of the waking state. I know this because the effects of believing—suffering—are completely gone now when I dream. I'm no longer afraid to go to sleep as I used to be when I had night terrors. I no longer have "bad" dreams or nightmares. I love my dreams and I learn from them. They have no hold over me as they would when I used to believe.

Q: That's really interesting. Would you mind elaborating? As in what dreaming was like before and what it's like for you now?
A: When I believed in the waking state, I carried that belief with me to the dreaming state. It's like belief was a primary function of who I was. Now that I say that, it *was* who I was—I was believing the story of me into existence.

When I was dreaming, this believing could lead to fear or even terror, or more typically in my case, anxiety. For me the recurring theme was finding myself completely unprepared for a major simulator evaluation—that is, the checkride—powerless to prevent myself from certain failure. Or I might be seated at a grand piano, in front of an audience of thousands, while I know for certain I couldn't play a single piece from beginning to end without drawing a blank and freezing.

When waking up from dreams, especially the powerful ones, for a few lingering seconds of disorientation, I'd find myself scrambling to reconstruct a reality to hold on to.

Where am I? (This question didn't have an obvious answer for me, because as a pilot—especially back when I used to fly out of Europe—I could be at home or more often at some hotel and usually in some other country.)

What time is it?

What's important in my life now? (This question brought forth the practical issues that I was thinking about the night before: Problems with varying degrees of significance that typically had something to do with money, health, or family.)

So I was this person, located somewhere (usually a hotel room), at some point in time (usually in the morning), with some problems that needed my attention (some minor, some serious).

I'd have this reality reconstructed in a matter of seconds, but as it was being assembled, I'd experience an uncomfortable limbo in which pretty much anything goes. I could be twenty years old. I could be ninety. I could be in a colony on Mars.

Usually, the deeper and more powerful the dream, the deeper the confusion when I transitioned to the waking state.

The greatest and most unsettling disorientation typically arose if I was exhausted and ended up napping in the middle of the day for more than two hours.

At some point in my life, it hit me that this "reality" I was waking into was nothing more than a story I'd constructed from thought.

This was a powerful realization: *"Reality" is just a construct built from thought.*

In the dream world, I could be me, I could be someone else. I could be a bodiless observer, like the reader of a book, watching the dream-story unfold. I could be a woman in the time of Jesus, or a man walking with Aristotle.

I'd believe a dream, no matter how radically it was untethered from my waking-state experience.

The main connection between the dream world and the waking-state world was the act of believing. In both cases, I believed.

Now dreams are just a continuation of experience. I look forward to sleeping and dreaming. If I lucid dream, that's great, and afterward I'll write down what I experienced. If I don't lucid dream, that's great too, and if I remember—I don't always—I'll record what I can to the best of my ability.

In writing out the dreams, I marvel at their wondrous fiction and more so at how easily I used to switch from believing my dream was real to believing the waking state was real.

Now I don't believe either is real and I enjoy both more than ever before.

Q: Why do you write down your dreams?
A: Oh, that's a carryover from when I started to lucid dream. It's a useful technique and leads to more-frequent lucid dreams. Also, it hones my writing skills because of the challenge of writing a dream as close to how I experienced it as possible.

Lucid Dreaming

Q: I'm fascinated by this idea of lucid dreaming. Do you lucid dream all the time?
A: No. It happens when it happens. If I put my attention on it before I sleep, it tends to happen more often. It also happens frequently during the lighter sleep of the morning.

Q: Is it possible to use the ITTIL technique when you're dreaming?
A: Absolutely.

Like with the waking state, the dream state can be seen to be untrue.

This is lucid dreaming.

Lucid dreaming occurs when you are aware you are dreaming.

There are degrees of lucidity, ranging from a vague feeling to the ability to control your dream world to the transcendental (knowingly transcending the dream itself).

Robert Waggoner has written numerous excellent books on the subject, all of which have been of great use and value to me. Lucid dreaming can be viewed as a kind of application of ITTIL in the dream state. There are many techniques for maintaining lucidity while dreaming, and Mr. Waggoner offers these in his writings as well (see Suggested Reading at the end of this book).

Lucid dreaming is a form of awakening within a dream. ITTIL is an awakening within the so-called "waking state."

When either the waking state or the dream state is seen to be a construct of thought and therefore not true, belief drops away and this allows the freedom of finding benefit in the dream or not.

When there is lucidity in dreaming, there is an awareness that it is a dream and, in my experience, more often than not, a strong willingness to maintain the dream state for all that it can offer. So even though I know it's a dream, I can still remain in the dream and use it and enjoy it for as long as it is beneficial to me, and for as long as I know I'm dreaming. If a lucid dream stops becoming beneficial, I wake up immediately. Actually, in order to remain lucid, I've noticed my attention is focused on the benefit of the dream.

If I'm aware I'm dreaming, the dream becomes anything I want it to be. I can use it any way I please.

Lucid dreams are a wonderful experiential metaphor for using thoughts without believing them.

I find dreams can be both fun and informative. It seems when I'm lucid dreaming that this sense of the potential in dreams is understood. If the dream is beneficial, I use it. Depending on my level of lucidity, I can manipulate the setting or even conjure people. Even at lesser degrees of lucidity, I can recognize the importance of certain events.

This often happens whenever there is an encounter with my father. I realize at the moment that I'm dreaming, and I have an opportunity to chat with my dad and I keep my attention on him and on any questions I might want to ask him.

I don't believe the dream is reality.

I simply know I'm dreaming and, more often than not, the dream is highly beneficial to me. It can be powerful on an emotional level, or informative, or simply fun.

If I'm aware that I'm dreaming and I decide to fly around, I don't believe I'm really flying around or that this is reality, but it still feels wonderful.

There is no fear in lucid dreams, because nothing in them is believed to be real, but I have found lucid dreaming can be a wonderful experience on many levels.

Dreams within Dreams

Q: What about dreams within dreams?

A: Most of us have had dreams where we wake up and realize we're still dreaming.

I've had dreams in which I'm actually talking about lucid dreaming without realizing that I'm actually in a dream!

Transposed to the waking state, this is a perfect example of the thought-system trap.

Thought can never think itself into being true. Thoughts tell lies that can never be disproven.

The only way out of this trap is to stop believing your thoughts.

In dreams, it's the realization, *I am dreaming*, that frees you from the weight of a dream and allows you to use the dream if you choose to or drop it (by waking up).

In the waking state, believing your thoughts is like being trapped in a dream.

The ITTIL technique awakens you and frees you from the weight of believing your thoughts so that you can use thoughts or drop them, in the same way a lucid dreamer can use a dream or choose to wake up.

SEEING STARS

Q: Are the stars we are seeing really there?

A: That's a philosophical question if I've ever heard one.

The ITTIL technique would change this thought into a statement and then find the opposite thought:

The stars we are seeing are really there. Not true.

The stars we are seeing are *not* really there. Not true.

According to science, the light that is seen from the closest star (other than the sun), Proxima Centauri, departed its source 14.25 years ago. The light from the nearest galaxy, Andromeda, left its source more than 2.5 million years ago.

Therefore from the perspective of the stars, we are actually observing their distant past.

It is possible that distant stars that we are seeing may no longer even exist.

Your question is loaded with assumptions that are untrue. First it assumes that there is an objective external world and we are separate, subjective observers of said observable world. It assumes that the stars can exist or not exist independently of the observer. So although the observer thinks light from a star is being seen, all there is, is the seeing. Conditioned thought steps in to say the seeing is of light and the light is coming from a star. Conventional thinking would lead to the conclusion that there really *is* a star. Another idea might postulate the possibility that the star has moved or no longer currently exists.

Immaterialism would say the star exists only as a thought. A realist may be assuming the star exists and moves in an objective reality, independent of the observer.

None of these ideas meets the definition of truth.

The ITTIL question is not whether a thought is true or not—and certainly not whether one thought is truer than another—the question is which untrue thought is more beneficial at this moment, and the answer to that depends on the thinker.

Any of these thoughts could be of practical value to someone at some time.

For the astronaut in a future I love to imagine, using a formula that assumes a movement of stars and planets to plot a course might be considered of great practical value in a situation where warp drive has been invented!

WHAT ABOUT NOW?

Q: Lots of spiritual teachers talk about presence. You talk about the present moment. But if no thought is true, then is there such a thing as a now?

A: Great question. Easy answer.

There is such a thing as a now. Not true.

There is *no* such thing as a now. Not true.

You get to pick which untrue thought is of benefit to you . . . well, at this present moment.

Time is relative and is therefore untrue. As you said, in some circles, the present moment is thought of as a given and is considered the only real time—everything that occurs, occurs now. I use this thought all the time, but I don't believe it.

For there to be a now, there must be a past and a future that define it. Therefore, in order for there to be a now, there must be time in the first place. The dictionary definition of now is "at the present moment in time." And so the concept of now exists within the concept of time, and time is relative and therefore not true by the definition given in this book.

Even if we disregard this, how can a now be defined?

Since *now*, by definition, is a moment in time (the present moment) then it should be possible to answer the following question:

Exactly when is now?

Is it this minute?

This second?

This millisecond?

This nanosecond?

By the time it takes thought to determine a now, that now is already in the past. Every thought believed to be of the present is actually always of the past. While thoughts may be said to arise in this now, thoughts about now are thoughts about the past (albeit a very recent one).

The benefit of a now is as obvious as its relativity. Fortunately, even science doesn't deny the relativity of time, and for the most part time is regarded as a tool.

That said, most people believe in the past.

The fundamental belief that most of us carry is that the past makes us what we are.

IS THE PAST HISTORY NOW?

Q: Whoa. You're saying the past doesn't exist? If the past doesn't exist, how can anything exist?

A: Again, I don't answer questions that seek truth, because I cannot offer truth. What I can offer is the ITTIL technique.

So using the technique, we have:

- The past exists. Not true.
- The past does *not* exist. Not true.

And:

- Nothing exists. Not true.
- Nothing does *not* exist. Not true.

Are any of these statements beneficial at the moment? That's the main question of value to you.

Q: Right, but you've skipped the supporting reasoning. Can you give me an example of supporting reasoning disproving a past?

A: Sure, but remember, the reasoning used has to resonate with *you* and the best person to find such reasoning can only be you. My reasoning is just as untrue as yours or as that of the greatest philosopher or scientist. The purpose of any reasoning is to see the original thought and its opposite as equally untrue. Once you find that balance, stop. Don't allow yourself to be convinced of the opposite thought!

So here it goes: We have seen that any thought that claims to be of the present is actually of the past.

But does the past even exist? Can there even be a past?

The past is defined as "having existed or taken place in a period before the present."

However, any thought of the past occurs in the hypothetical now (I say hypothetical because we have seen that the thought that says there's a now is not true). We cannot be aware of a thought of the past that is occurring in the past (or in the future), because within the relativistic construct of time, all thoughts are said to arise in the present moment—in the now (whatever that is).

So within the framework of time, thoughts of the past only ever occur in the hypothetical now. Therefore, there is no past other than what is being thought of as a past in the present.

There is no evidence to support the existence of a past, since time itself is a relative construct and therefore untrue.

Thoughts that use the idea of a past without believing in a past can be beneficial, however. For instance, thoughts that use some idea, method, or technique learned in the past for application in the present.

Thoughts that suggest there is a past might also be seen as not beneficial. Such thoughts may include "I should have done better," or "I made a terrible mistake."

Most people would agree there's no point in crying over proverbial spilled milk. Likewise, most people would also agree that great value can be derived in the lessons learned from the past.

The idea of a past is of immeasurable value. While this might be obvious, what may not be so obvious is the role belief plays.

The vast majority of people believe in a past. They use the idea, but they also treat it as though it were an unquestionable truth.

There is a past. Not true.

There is *not* a past. Not true.

Belief in a past can be the source of great suffering.

If I were to believe there really is a past, then I place my perception of myself on this imaginary timeline and bundle it in the same truth-package I call *my* past.

This past constitutes a major part of my identity. I've learned how to play the piano and how to fly airplanes, and I can apply that knowledge whenever it is useful. On the other hand, this belief can mean I also screwed this or that up, experienced such and such tragedies, and the mess that is my history is sustained in my belief. Now I have "baggage."

The past doesn't have to be negative, of course—I could be remembering only the "good" things.

Either way, it's a story and it's not true. Identifying myself with a lie is going to cause pain, whether it's a pleasant fairy tale or an R-rated nightmare.

It is essential to clarify that the statement "There is not a past" is equally untrue.

Applying the ITTIL technique, I can use either statement regarding the past without the detriment of belief, if it appears to be beneficial at the moment.

Without believing in a past or no past, I am free to use any thought related to a past or no past that is beneficial to me at any moment.

And since I see clearly that both a past and no past are equally untrue, the instant a past-related thought is no longer beneficial to me, it can be discarded.

I only give myself a history if and when it's beneficial to me. I don't believe in stories, not even the story of "me."

By the way, it is interesting to note that in Greek, the word "history" and "story" are the same.

FALSE LOGIC

Q: If, as you say, we have to end all belief, how do we tackle things that are just plain true, like logic in math?
A: It only seems difficult when you believe you are dealing with truth.

Logic is a sticky belief for many. After all, math and science are based on it.

A leads to *B*.

B leads to *C*.

Both are given as true.

Thus, *A* leads to *C*.

This is fundamental logic.

Two elements have rules that can be applied to them—you can have *A* or *B*.

In order to derive any truth from logic, there need to be assumptions that are given as true. But *logic cannot prove the initial assumption*. How can you use logic to prove truths, when logic cannot prove the original assumptions upon which it is founded?

In other words, logic is used to prove truths, but in order to apply the logic, you need to have something "true" to work with. Since it is not possible to get this truth through logic, then it follows that logic cannot prove anything to be true.

It's basically building a tower on sand.

Mathematical logic, being based on assumptions, fails to satisfy the ITTIL definition of truth.

The only question is not of validity, but of its value to you right now.

Others may find logic useful. Obviously, just imagine asking Mr. Spock!

(You'd probably get the same answer from a mathematician, engineer, or scientist.)

Again, in the practice of ITTIL, the utility of an idea stands on its own without there being a need to believe in its validity.

Imaginary Numbers

Q: Can you give another example in math of something useful and at the same time not true?

A: Yes—imaginary numbers. It is clear, by definition, that they are just that: imaginary.

While untrue, imaginary numbers are useful. They are used in complex number theory, which is useful in mathematics, science, and especially engineering.

Just for one example, whose usefulness I can corroborate personally, complex number theory is used in producing more fuel-efficient airplane wings, such as the ones on the new Boeing 787 Dreamliner.

1 + 1

Q: All right, so what about 1 + 1? Everyone knows the answer to that. How can that be untrue as well?

A: Right off the bat, our schooling and conditioning has us think of the equation 1 + 1 = 2.

So just by seeing 1 + 1, conditioning gives 1 + 1 = 2.

In fact, calculators and calculator apps often spew out an immediate summation of these numbers, giving a result of 2 before you even have a chance to tap on the enter key.

But let's take a step back, look at 1 + 1, and see the assumptions made here.

What is 1?

It is the symbolic representation of the number one.

What is a number?

The dictionary defines a *number* as "a word or symbol that represents a quantity."

So far, so good, right?

What is +?

The dictionary defines the + symbol as follows: "used to indicate that one number or amount is being added to another."

If one number—in your question, the number 1—can be added to another, then, by definition, there can be more than one. A nondual perspective on this equation might be 1 + 1 = 1.

In philosophy, it can be argued that just saying "one" implies the possibility of more than one. But 1 + 1 = 2 brings home the point clearly enough on its own.

The point is this: *the language of mathematics, like any other language, is dualistic.*

Mathematics is said to be the language of truth, but this cannot be true according to the definition of truth given in this book.

The language of mathematics is dualistic.

Duality has an opposite, nonduality.

Therefore the language of mathematics is not true because it fails the first requirement of truth according to the principles of ITTIL: truth has no opposite.

Q: Yes, but the language of mathematics is only untrue under your definition of truth, and you yourself said your definition of truth is not true.

A: Yes. No statement in this book can be true, even the one regarding truth itself.

That's not the point. The point is deconstructing the belief in any truth that can be known by thought. Since belief is born of thought and the reasoning that supports it, and since no thought can be true, by extension, no belief can be true.

With belief, there is suffering.

Freeing thought from belief, you can use thought without suffering.

That is the point.

As far as the ITTIL definition of truth goes, even the language of mathematics is not true.

Again, a thought doesn't have to be true for it to be of benefit. And if it is believed to be true, then its benefit is offset by the suffering that is caused by believing it.

Q: How does believing 1 + 1 = 2 cause suffering?

A: Now, that's a great question.

It's not believing 1 + 1 = 2 in particular that causes suffering (at least, not directly), it's believing *itself* that causes suffering.

In order for there to be freedom from suffering, there has to be freedom from *all* belief, including believing that 1 + 1 = 2.

THE PATHLESS PATH

Q: You say the ITTIL technique is not a path. I have heard of something called the pathless path. Can you talk about that?

A: Yes. There is a path in the sense that there is action. It is pathless, because the action doesn't lead anywhere—there is no imagined future destination. The destination is the action in the moment.

The moment the ITTIL technique is practiced, there is an awakening in the now—in the present. In this way the path—the practice of the ITTIL technique—and the goal—awakening now—are one.

The sand mandala is the perfect metaphor for the pathless path. It is a gorgeous work of art, created grain by grain, and the final result is destroyed as a part of the ritual.

It is normally seen as a metaphor for the transitory nature of life.

But there is another way of looking at it—knowing that the product of the path, the goal, will be destroyed the moment it is attained, the goal has no importance. What then becomes important is the action taken in the moment to achieve the goal. In this case, the laying of each colored grain.

The goal is important only in the act of laying the grain. Lost in the moment—in the art of creating the mandala—the goal is not the purpose as with most paths. The action in the moment is the purpose, there is no future to look upon, and the intense focus allows no room for a past either.

PRESENCE

Q: Does the pathless path relate in any way to presence?

A: Yes, very much so.

I was on the treadmill one morning and I had a funny thought: "What would someone from a primitive society with no technology think if he were to observe me running in place on this crazy device, expending all this energy and yet getting nowhere?"

In our not-too-distant past, running served the very practical purpose of getting from A to B as quickly as possible on foot. Presumably when other means of transportation, such as a horse, were not readily available.

That morning, I was running on a treadmill simply for the sake of running. Not to get from A to B, prepare for a marathon, or even to lose weight. And since I was running in place, there was no beautiful scenery to observe either.

There was no goal, there was just running.

Present with my body in the act of running without projecting into some imaginary future goal, I noticed that I enjoyed what I was doing without feeling like I was doing anything at all—almost as if I were moving yet completely still.

I finally understood then what my wife meant by a "runner's high."

It is presence. In this case, stillness in action.

FIGHTING PARADOX

Q: All this seems highly paradoxical. How do you fight paradox?
A: Fighting paradox is the same as trying to find truth using reasoning. There is no solution to an unsolvable puzzle.

The temptation is to say, "Just because I cannot come up with proof, it doesn't mean there isn't proof out there waiting to be discovered someday."

Whether or not you see that this kind of thinking cannot arrive at a satisfactory conclusion, you will eventually realize that it isn't *beneficial*.

Why? Simply because all it does is lead to more thinking.

It is being stuck in an unsolvable puzzle using thinking, but when used this way, thought becomes the puzzle itself.

Also, and more important, the point of the ITTIL technique isn't to resolve any puzzle or paradox or to find any answers, it's to use thoughts without the suffering caused by believing them.

In this state of peace, questions about fighting paradox simply don't arise, because the source of the problem itself—believing thought—is now a thing of the past.

EMBRACING PARADOX

Q: If fighting paradox is futile, what is the solution?

A: Short answer: Use the ITTIL technique and don't treat it as a philosophy. By using it as a technique, you will come to embrace paradox.

No belief can be reasoned to an irrefutable conclusion. Nothing can be proven. So the opposite of the belief will always come forth in the form of doubt. A doubt that never offers resolution, because even the doubt itself cannot be proven.

"I Think, Therefore I Lie" is a paradox.

Instead of trying to unravel that statement and prove it true or untrue, use it merely as a tool that serves as a technique. Then there will be no paradox to contend with.

The practice of the ITTIL technique leads to freedom of thought in the realm of paradox. This embracing of paradox is what comes naturally from embracing all opposites without belief. It is a state of complete acceptance.

By embracing paradox, you don't find yourself in a state of constant unsettled confusion. Actually, the experience is quite the opposite.

This is because it isn't paradox (or thought) that causes constant unsettling confusion, it is belief, and with ITTIL belief is no longer part of the thinking process.

In that space, there is peace.

EMBRACING ALL OPPOSITES

Q: Okay, so if you're using the ITTIL technique and embracing paradox, aren't you trying to function with one foot in one statement and the other planted in the opposite statement? Doesn't this lead to a kind of analysis paralysis?

A: Not at all.

When all belief is dropped, the ITTIL process is automatic, and what follows is a complete openness to everything.

What once seemed like the most opposed thoughts no longer remain in opposition. On the level of reasoning, they oppose, but *reason is the language of belief.*

Thoughts no longer oppose because there is nothing to oppose them. All opposites are now embraced.

The statement that all thoughts are true *and* all thoughts are not true is no longer seen as a contradiction.

Without belief, the deepest paradox is embraced completely.

And though this may seem confusing, it is only so if you use reasoning to support belief.

With belief out of the equation, embracing all opposites is a paradox experienced in an exquisite marriage of chaos and harmony, at the foundation of which is an ever-expanding grace and gratitude.

A vibrant and glorious peace.

USING THE ITTIL TECHNIQUE WITH OTHER TECHNIQUES

Q: Is it okay to use the ITTIL technique with other techniques or paths?

A: Definitely. It blends in with any technique, path, or religion.

While I was still discovering the ITTIL technique, I often found that it is fun to experience other things, and I continue to do so now.

I don't see other techniques or paths as leading to truth or some goal. I don't carry any belief, nor do I resist, even when some path or technique calls for belief. I process what is being said without believing and move on.

This may sound difficult and confusing, but, in my experience, this is not at all the case. In the openness that is release from belief, all things flow easily.

I don't see there being anything true. No thought, and by extension, no technique or path.

My constant remains what is beneficial at this moment.

Q: What About the Direct Path?
A: The Direct Path is a way of stepping behind thought and using direct experience to discern truth.

This method doesn't help with thoughts, it sidesteps them entirely. This can be a wonderful way to unveil truth and would serve as a perfect complement to the ITTIL technique, especially for people who have advanced to where they are no longer believing negative psychological thoughts.

The Direct Path uses thought in order to go beyond thought, but from what I know about it, there isn't some easy technique to apply. The end result may be the same, but the Direct Path may not resonate with everyone, nor does it necessarily yield immediate results.

COUNSELING

Q: Since I have the ITTIL technique, should I stop seeing my shrink?
A: If you are deriving benefit from seeing a therapist, why stop? Especially if you are seeing a therapist for serious psychological issues or trauma.

But let's say you're seeking a therapist to work on less serious issues. Using the ITTIL technique we have:

"I should stop seeing my shrink." Not true.

"I should *not* stop seeing my shrink." Not true.

As long as you're not believing either thought, again, it boils down to whether seeing your shrink or not is beneficial to you.

The ITTIL technique is not about self-improvement, seeing a good therapist for minor issues is. The story of you, like any story, can always be improved upon, if you find it beneficial.

Personally, I have been seeing a counselor for some years now, and I continue to do so when I feel it is beneficial. There is no story or belief around this. There's no expectation of finding a solution, because there is no problem. There's just the continuous learning process.

I choose to view counseling as a tool for growth rather than thinking of it as a way to solve a problem. To support this view, the word "counseling"—giving advice—seems to fit better than "therapy," which sounds exclusively limited to resolving problems, but is—from my perspective, of course—way better than "seeing a shrink." Again, I think it's important to emphasize here that I say this within the context of seeing a therapist for minor issues, not major problems or trauma.

Our family has been blessed with a wonderful counselor. We have learned—and continue to learn—so much from him in the area of relationships.

Counseling has been beneficial to us for more than five years now. I haven't once left his office without learning something new about relating to others.

I highly recommend counseling as a tool for as long as you find it beneficial. If you're happy with the shrink you have, then more power to you. If not, I recommend setting the bar high and finding the best counselor for you and your family (if you have one). In our case, it took a lot of searching and determination before we found the right person to help us.

Even if it proves to be as hard for you to find the right match as it was for us, I think you'll find it's well worth the time and effort.

TRANSCENDENTAL MEDITATION

Q: You mentioned early on that you practiced TM. How has that been beneficial to you?

A: Transcendental Meditation (TM) was introduced to me when I was in my mid-teens. It couldn't have come at a better time. I was overthinking and overanalyzing everything. Using the power of thought I tried to protect myself from the world and the frightening future I imagined.

To say that TM was a blessing would be a colossal understatement.

I have been practicing TM since 1981, and it has always been effortless and it always worked. It can never not work. If it doesn't work or if effort is required, then it isn't TM, it's something else.

During the practice of TM, thoughts are not important.

So for me, it was like pressing the Pause button on all the drama that was my life.

While meditating, the compulsion to latch on to thoughts and give them importance was gone. The experience of transcending thoughts gave rise to a direct experience that I am not my thoughts, thereby negating the belief in the idea that says, I think, therefore I am.

It is possible that the long-term practice of TM may have also led to my stepping back from day-to-day thoughts, leading me to eventually regard thought as a tool, rather than as a means for knowing truth.

COMING FROM THE HEART

Q: I have practiced the ITTIL technique for some time and I'm a lot less bothered by things in life, but I feel detached more than I feel connected. I don't feel like I'm operating from the heart at all. Am I doing something wrong?

A: No. Everyone's experience of awakening in the moment is different. If your practice of ITTIL leaves you free from belief and you are awakened in the moment, you are open to whatever arises now.

That arising may or may not feel like an opening on the level of the heart. It may even feel extraordinarily ordinary! You asked if you were doing something wrong. It's not helpful for you to think of your experiences of the ITTIL technique as right or wrong. If you are suffering in any way, then simply continue to apply the ITTIL technique. If you are not suffering, then simply allow that blessing without any expectations for anything more. That comparison, expectation, or longing—even for something as sublime and beautiful as operating from the level of the heart—will plunge you back to seeking and to rejection of the present moment.

Q: This is all about the intellect, not the heart. But life isn't just thinking.
A: When people say heart, it's a metaphor for love or loving. Either that, or they're referring to loving thoughts and they claim they come from the heart. Unconditional love is beyond thoughts. To operate from that level you first need to be free from bondage to thought—free from belief, otherwise operating from the level of the heart either won't take place or it will only happen for short rare instances because belief will creep in and move attention to thoughts and hold on to them. That process, no matter if the thoughts are of love or loving, is not what is meant by operating from the heart. To operate at that level, you must first be free of all belief. To be free of all belief, you need ITTIL. This is why ITTIL is at the core of what is being offered.

ENLIGHTENMENT AND AWAKENING

Q: You say your goal as a teenager was to become enlightened. What happened with that? Did you ever achieve that goal? I mean, the only time you mention enlightenment is when you talk about your past aspirations. When you talk about more-recent years, you use the word *awakening*. Isn't "awakening" just another word for "enlightenment"?

A: It can be, but that would depend on your definition of enlightenment.

Until fairly recently, I used the word *enlightenment* in the sense of becoming lighter by unloading the beliefs in the moment. But this interpretation required constant explaining, because most people view enlightenment as something much more—a kind of state from which all negative experiences are held at a lofty distance. Something . . . well . . . almost unattainable. This is the way I thought of enlightenment when I was a teenager and for many decades thereafter. So that's why I use the word enlightenment instead of awakening when I refer back to those times when I thought of becoming enlightened as a goal.

In the context of how I used to think of enlightenment—as in becoming enlightened—the word enlightenment carried with it an idea of permanence.

Someone being enlightened is a story about a person—that is, something transitory and therefore unreal—acquiring something permanent and real.

That which is real, simply is. It isn't acquired, nor can it be known by anything unreal. Truth cannot be known by a lie.

Truth simply is.

Truth is what is left when belief in a lie is gone. It is not found, for there is nothing to find it. It stands on its own, unknowable by thought.

When the veil of belief is lifted, truth is revealed unto itself in an awakening that happens right now.

I no longer find the story of becoming enlightened beneficial, primarily because it perpetuates seeking. This story also turns the word enlightenment into a permanent state and goal to be attained in the future, and for that reason I've stopped using the word enlightenment in association with the ITTIL technique.

I don't see awakening as being synonymous with enlightenment, at least not with what seems to be the common definition of enlightenment. Awakening is coming out of a dream and into the reality of what is.

Q: Yes, but a lot of spiritual teachers use "awakening" and "enlightenment" interchangeably. They define both as the end of suffering, the end of seeking, or sometimes both—which is pretty much what you're saying about awakening. Since you say that ITTIL has become automatic for you and that the technique awakens you, then aren't you indirectly saying you're enlightened?

A: No, but nice try!

The ITTIL technique awakens you to the *present moment*. It is for awakening *now*. That is very different from saying the ITTIL technique is for permanent future awakening, enlightenment, liberation, self-realization, or whatever expression you want to use.

So do I tell myself or others that I've achieved my childhood goal of becoming enlightened?

No. I don't even have that goal anymore, thank God! What a burden that was—striving for something I'd made as impossible as it was undefinable.

Though the ITTIL technique is automatic for me now, and I haven't suffered or sought truth or happiness outside the present moment, it is conceivable that I might at some point in the future.

Being open in the present moment doesn't mean that openness is restricted to things that are considered pleasant only! Otherwise, that wouldn't be openness. And so being open, even to the possibility of something like seeking and suffering, is part of the very nature of complete openness—it doesn't discriminate, it loves whatever arises unconditionally.

This perspective comes from the untrue thought that I do *not* have choice.

From the perspective of the equally untrue thought that I *do* have choice, why would I choose to suffer? Why would I choose to seek truth or happiness when they are ever-present right now?

I can't think of a reason that suffering and seeking would benefit me, but at the same time, I can't predict the future either.

Who knows, maybe I will choose suffering one day.

All I can say is that while it's possible, it doesn't seem probable.

Q: To be honest, it sounds to me like you gave up on your dream and stopped short of your goal of becoming enlightened. For those of us like me, who haven't given up, do you think the ITTIL technique helps along the path to becoming enlightened?

A: I agree that I have dropped the goal of becoming enlightened. The way I see it, though, there's a difference between *letting go* of something that's not beneficial and *giving up* on something that is. The story of becoming enlightened no longer served me after I found ITTIL. It was of great benefit in the beginning, because the searching eventually led to the discovery of the ITTIL technique.

I didn't give up on a dream or settle for less—I let go of a fantasy of a better, happier future in favor of embracing the blessing of what is.

Once I stopped the search for happiness, truth, and my idea of enlightenment, I was open to awakening now.

I've never experienced seeking and presence at the same time, have you?

Therefore, I see no benefit in the notion of becoming enlightened.

Ironically, it is the desire to become enlightened that keeps you from being enlightened in the moment.

To answer your question, will ITTIL help you become enlightened?

No, it won't.

This is because when practicing the technique, the story of you becoming enlightened—as in attaining a permanent state—would be dissolved along with all the other stories and beliefs that are muddying your clarity in the present moment.

ITTIL is a technique that gives you the *choice* to awaken now.

The ITTIL technique came to me after years of inquiry. Before then, I had no choice but to suffer and seek because I had no options.

There were no practical alternatives to suffering and seeking that I could apply at any time.

After the ITTIL technique, I had the *choice* to awaken to what is, or suffer and continue seeking truth and happiness outside the present moment.

This is the choice that is being offered to you now.

The ITTIL technique stands on its own.

You don't need to keep chasing enlightenment.

Let experience be your guide.

Don't take my word for it or anyone else's.

Look for answers nowhere.

Live your direct experience.

That experience, without belief, is awakening now.

Suggested Reading

The following books were especially valuable to me in helping deconstruct certain deep-rooted beliefs that were grounded in duality.

Atmananda, Sri. *Atma Darshan/Atma Nirvriti.* Soquel, CA: Advaita Publishers, 1983. This is what I consider the Direct Path bible. Powerful, short.

Berkeley, George. *Principles of Human Knowledge and Three Dialogues.* Edited by Roger Woolhouse. New York: Penguin, 1988. Written in eighteenth-century English, but very clear for its time. A great introduction to immaterialism.

Goode, Greg. *The Direct Path—A User Guide.* Salisbury, UK: Nonduality Press, 2012. A practice that brings nonduality to the level of experience.

Goode, Greg. *Standing As Awareness.* Salisbury, UK: Nonduality Press, 2009. A wonderful book on nonduality.

Harding, Douglas. *On Having No Head: Zen and the Rediscovery of the Obvious.* Agoura Hills, CA: Inner Directions Press, 2002. Hilarious. Lovely. Totally in-your-face, upside-down thinking that dislodges even the most unquestionable "facts."

Waggoner, Robert. *Lucid Dreaming: Gateway to the Inner Self.* Needham, MA: Moment Point Press, 2009. One of my favorite books on the topic. Simple and deep.

Watzlawick, Paul. *The Invented Reality: How Do We Know What We Believe We Know.* New York: W. W. Norton, 1984. A series of essays, some easier to read than others, but all of them highly beneficial.

Acknowledgments

First and foremost, I would like to thank my copyeditor, Rachelle Mandik, for her tremendous help with making this lifework a reality. I have said it before and I'll say it again: Rachelle is simply amazing.

Rachelle introduced me to Neil Gordon, whose insights into restructuring the content of this book were invaluable. Thanks, Neil!

Thanks also to concept editor Pauline Zavitzianos for helping me remain clear, simple, and on message.

As always, Alex Z was a great help keeping my logic straight.

Debra Nichols has a remarkable eye for detail, and she deserves a standing ovation for the work she has done proofreading and editing both the first and second editions of this book.

I'd also like to thank Karen Minster, my interior book designer, who took on the great challenge of making this book flow visually in a way that is both effective and appealing.

Thanks also to Laura Duffy who did a superb job putting the essential final touches on the original book cover designed by Eric Hubbel.

I'd like to thank my beloved wife, Chloe. She has been a tremendous help in making sure the message was as clear as possible from beginning to end.

Made in the
USA
Monee, IL